SCHOLASTIC

Just-Right Writing Mini-Lessons

Grades 4–6

Mini-Lessons to Teach Your Students the Essential Skills and Strategies They Need to Write Fiction and Nonfiction

Cheryl M. Sigmon and Sylvia M. Ford

New York • Toronto • London • Auckland • Sydney
Mexico City • New Delhi • Hong Kong • Buenos Aires

Teaching *Resources*

DEDICATION

How lucky we were to have Joanna Davis-Swing and Merryl Maleska Wilbur as our editors again!

Joanna, you've guided this project with endless optimism and gentle wisdom.
You are a true hero and we so greatly admire you!

Merryl, as always, you've shown utmost patience, the most careful eye, and an insightful mind. There were so many instances where you went far beyond what should have been expected of an editor.

Our sincerest gratitude again to both of you ladies who've not only made our jobs a pleasure but who've also made this whole series a great resource for teachers!

CMS and SMF

To Don, with all my love—Thanks for your patience and understanding, for eating leftovers and take-out, for buying fresh flowers to boost my spirits, and for always believing in me.

SMF

To Ray, my dance and life partner . . . you enrich my life at every turn.

CMS

ACKNOWLEDGEMENTS FOR WRITING SAMPLES AND PHOTOGRAPHS

Cheryll Hallum, Principal, and Debra Havens, Sandra Riley, and other teachers at
Benjamin Franklin Science Academy, Muskogee, OK; and Peggy Jones,
Director of Professional Development, Muskogee School District, Muskogee, OK

Lara Crowley and Debbie Panchisin, Curriculum Consultants,
Appoquinimink School District, Odessa, DE

Joy Dewing and Leslie Lewis, Central Middle School, Kokomo, IN

Lisa Gilpin, Sand Creek Elementary School, North Vernon, IN

Ann Hollar, Horace Mann Elementary School, Huntington, IN

Kay Kinder, Coordinator of Instructional Services; Cindy Dwyer, Principal, Bon Air;
Brian VanBuskirk, Principal, Central; Sharon Hahn, Principal, Columbian; Paula Concus,
Principal, Darrough Chapel; Claudette Renfro, Principal, Pettit Park; Linda Campbell, Principal,
Washington: Kokomo-Center Township Consolidated School Corporation, Kokomo, IN

Todd Leininger and upper grade teachers, North Miami Elementary School, Denver, IN

Barbara Steele, Principal, Northside Elementary School, Colleton County School District, Walterboro, SC

Linda Gillespie and Deborah Green-Wilson, Title One Office; Richard Moore, Principal, and
Nan Gray, Curriculum Resource Teacher, Logan Elementary; Delores Gilliard, Principal, and Kitty Faden,
Curriculum Resource Teacher, Greenview Elementary School; Liz Eason, Principal, and
Presphonia Perkins, Curriculum Resource Teacher, Hyatt Park Elementary School,
Richland School District One, Columbia, SC

Tony Ross, Principal, and Sally Mills, fifth-grade teacher, 6th District Elementary School, Covington, KY

Cover design by Jason Robinson.
Cover photo by James Levin.
Interior design by Solutions by Design, Inc.
Interior photos courtesy of the authors.

ISBN-13: 978-0-439-57410-5
ISBN-10: 0-439-57410-2

1 2 3 4 5 6 7 8 9 10   40 12 11 10 09 08 07 06

Table of Contents

Introduction

How to Use This Book

This new book in our series of writing mini-lesson books shares the same goal as the earlier books: showing teachers how to integrate what needs to be taught into a powerful instructional context—real writing! Many of us were not taught how to write well when we were in school. We were given writing assignments, but our teachers rarely

instructed us about the attributes of quality writing. Additionally, real writing was something that we were only permitted to do after we learned the proper mechanics, grammar, and usage to express our thoughts and ideas correctly. Our grades often reflected the level of correctness we'd achieved, regardless of the originality or development of our ideas, the richness of our figurative language, or the voice in which we wrote.

Gone are those days! Educators now realize that assigning writing doesn't teach it. Instruction needs to be direct and explicit to have an impact on beginning writers, and it needs to be offered in the context of something that makes sense to students—the context of real writing. Teachers also realize that correctness of conventions doesn't make writing better—only cleaner. And clean writing and good writing don't always equate.

Modeling writing daily—showing rather than telling about the attributes of effective communication—leads students to those "aha!" moments of understanding: "That's why I need a comma after an introductory clause!" or "Those adjectives really help my character come alive!" or "Combining those sentences made all the difference!" We now know that daily modeling helps students transfer new knowledge to their own writing.

And so you'll find this to be a book of short, powerful daily lessons—sound bites, if you will—that teachers might model in the framework of a Writing Workshop. There is such power in the relatively brief time we dedicate to the daily mini-lesson. Our sincerest hope is that this book will help you take full advantage of that time.

How This Book Fits Into the Series

This book is a part of a series that began with a book for first-grade writers. That book deals with teaching students that writing is, above all else, a basic communication skill—anything that can be said can also be written. The little ones need to know that. They need to feel empowered to communicate at whatever level they're able to as they build confidence in themselves as writers.

Most of the models at that beginning level provide opportunities for students to share occurrences from their daily lives—the birth of a baby brother, a trip to the grocery store with Mom, a run they scored in a ball game, a visit to the veterinarian with their pet. These young students learn real-world contexts for writing—such as thank-you notes for gifts and invitations to parties—as well as the basic conventions of writing, such as capitalization and punctuation.

The second book in this series is aimed at grades 2–3. It picks up from many of the lessons in the first-grade book and also includes connections to math, science, and social studies because by these grades writing is already becoming a stronger tool for learning subject area content. The conventions taught are more technical and advanced. However, for grades 2–3, just as for first grade, personal narrative writing receives the greatest emphasis.

In this new book, for grades 4–6, you'll see a great deal more integration of writing and content area learning, as well as a strong reading and writing connection. Typically, intermediate-grade teachers need to juggle great demands stemming from curriculum standards in many different subject areas beyond language arts but do not receive additional time to achieve these myriad goals. Also at these grade levels, teachers may feel more accountability pressure from high-stakes testing programs.

When teachers know how to make writing an effective tool for their students, they accomplish a number of key goals at the same time. Not only do their students become better writers, they also become better learners. Teachers benefit directly as well because they can meet the curriculum demands more effectively. Researchers of best practice have shown that writing may be used successfully in all subject areas to activate students' prior knowledge, elicit questions that draw students into the subject, build comprehension, teach vocabulary, promote discussion, and encourage reflection (Zemelman et al., 1998). Thus, integration is critical. The lessons in this book demonstrate how teachers can make the most of integration while moving students toward more independence as writers.

For more mini-lessons based on science and social studies content, we invite you to refer to our book *Writing Lessons for the Content Areas* (Sigmon & Ford, 2005), which is closely related to this series. It is based on five essential tools for teaching writing in concert with content and works especially well in tandem with this book for grades 4–6.

This teacher provides her students with lots of time for real writing and engages them in frequent informal conversations about their writing.

How These Mini-Lessons Were Selected

Good instruction in the classroom is usually based on two things: (1) the needs of the students as evidenced by their writing and their conversations and (2) the curriculum provided by the school, district, or state that defines what students should know and be able to do at that particular grade level.

As the teacher, you may adapt the information in this book to your students' needs. If most of the students demonstrate a similar need, the instruction may become a mini-lesson for the entire class. If, instead, a particular student has a unique need, you may decide to provide one-on-one instruction during an individual conference with that student. We don't pretend to know your students well enough to suggest that there is a perfect match between the mini-lessons in this book and their specific needs. However, after many years of experience, we can assure you that, with some tweaking here and there, you'll be close!

Curriculum guides also inform teachers' decisions about mini-lessons. Most teachers believe that it would be foolish not to align instruction, curriculum, and district/state assessment. Hopefully, that curriculum includes criteria for good, quality writing.

In designing this guide, we reviewed the language arts curriculum guides of ten states around the country. We then mapped these standards to find the most common writing objectives—relevant to grades 4–6—shared among these ten states. Additionally, we used the state and national standards in the content areas of science and social studies for grades 4–6 as a context for some of the lessons.

Many of the lessons model how to weave together language arts and content area standards and objectives into instruction that feels natural and genuine. We attempt to show students how the use of these standards really does help their writing to be clearer and more powerful while at the same time giving them a way to process the content material in a more meaningful and engaging way. We hope that the mini-lessons serve to motivate students to write by letting them see how easy writing can be and how it can have a real effect on others.

> Along with the National Standards, the standards of the following ten states were gathered to create the curriculum for this book: California, Colorado, Florida, Indiana, New York, Pennsylvania, South Carolina, Texas, Virginia, and Washington.

Sequencing Your Lessons

The lessons in this book do not necessarily appear in the order in which you should teach them throughout the year. Instead they are organized by purpose. We recommend viewing the sections as a menu. You may pick and choose appropriately based on your students' needs and on opportunities to integrate lessons with other content being taught.

You will find that most of the daily lessons in this book can be used independent of subsequent lessons. For example, there are several types of poems taught throughout the book—bio poems, poems for two voices, and free verse poems. You may combine these lessons into a single poetry unit or use them at different times according to the content on which they're based. The table of contents will allow you to pick and choose according to your needs.

Here are some hints about designing the appropriate sequence of lessons in your classroom:

☆ At the very beginning of the year, we strongly suggest that you start off your Writing Workshop by giving your students daily opportunities to write about whatever they choose to write about. Once they develop confidence in themselves as writers, you can begin to do the more focused kind of writing included in these lessons.

☆ Keep in mind that although students in grades 4–6 have had instruction in basic writing conventions for years, you'll need to review these conventions—such as the Quick Check list (page 37)—early on. Daily writing opportunities, unfortunately, are not a uniform practice in all schools. So it's important to realize that for some students the mini-lessons in the basics are only a review, whereas for others the lessons are a true introduction to the Writing Workshop experience. Either way, not only will this review establish your own clear expectations, but it will help all students feel confident in their ability to write.

☆ "Section One: Planning for Writing" and "Section Two: Writing the Draft" include both lessons for the beginning of the school year as well as approaches for planning and writing more sophisticated pieces later in the year. Read through those lessons and decide—given your own classroom needs—which are practical for earlier in the year and which are more appropriate for later in the year.

☆ Mix in lessons from Sections Three through Six throughout the year as you feel they're appropriate to support your students' growth in writing. Be sure to think about balancing lessons that deal with conventions and those that deal with revisions.

☆ We definitely do not advise teaching all of the "Making Writing Cleaner and Clearer" lessons in Section Three in succession; doing so might convey to students that writing has to be correct to be acceptable or good. Mix lessons on grammar, mechanics, and usage with lessons from other sections.

☆ Lessons from "Section Five: Writing for a Variety of Purposes" should be sprinkled throughout the year so that students develop a clear understanding that writing has real applications in their everyday lives. We do not want students to view writing as handing in a set of assignments! Writing for real purposes and audiences provides enormous motivation to your students.

☆ Don't leave "Section Six: Polishing and Publishing Our Writing" until the end of the year. You'll quickly discover that publishing is, perhaps, the greatest motivator in getting students to want to produce quality writing. So read this section and use its ideas even in your first semester of instruction.

This wall of teachers' autobiographical collages offers a wonderful model for students' own writing.

We hope that the book will also give you good ideas for teaching content area curricula—social studies, science, math, health, and so on—in tandem with your language arts. As you read through the table of contents, think about your other content. Put together a scope and sequence of lessons that is tailored to your students' needs.

The Mini-Lesson as Part of the Writing Workshop

The Writing Workshop is traditionally divided into three parts: (1) the teacher's model lesson; (2) the students' writing time, including time for the teacher to work one-on-one with students; and (3) time for students to share their work. Although frequently we do include a step in the lesson outline that describes students' own writing time, this book focuses on the first segment—the direct instruction/ model lessons offered by the teacher. We recommend viewing the writing and sharing times quite

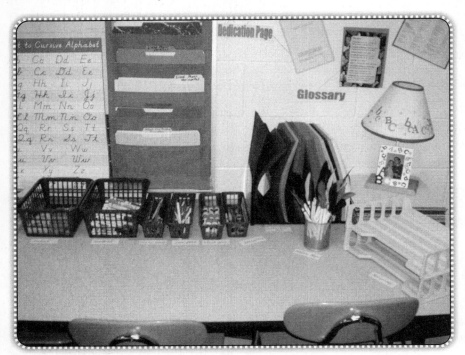

flexibly—often your model lessons will have a direct impact on students' work that day, but there is not always an expectation that students will write daily about what the teacher has written about or even that the targeted skill will be practiced that very day by the students. We have found that artificial, stilted writing can result from the expectation that students must immediately incorporate a new skill into their writing. Instead, our priority is for students to experience daily good writing instruction and then to put their new skills and knowledge to use as the need occurs in their own writing.

This sixth-grade writing center—well-organized, stocked with supplies, and attractively set-up—gives students a dedicated spot to work on their writing.

We especially use individual student-teacher conferences to encourage students to apply what they've been learning on an ongoing basis.

The first segment is a regular, daily session in which the teacher writes for students. Although some of the lessons may span multiple days, for each day this portion of the workshop should usually fit into a ten- to fifteen-minute framework. Modeling may be done in any number of ways; typically, however, it involves the teacher sitting down to write while the students observe. Because this serves as the teacher's direct, explicit instruction, it may not be as interactive as instruction during other parts of the day.

Our favorite way to model the daily writing is to sit down beside an overhead projector, simulating as closely as possible the posture students will assume during their writing time. We face the class, allowing the students to watch and listen as we make the decisions that writers make when they compose. Think of the following list of materials and resources as standard for a large number of the mini-lessons in this book. Within each lesson, we also include a brief list of materials and resources particular to that lesson's activity. Standard materials may include

☆ transparencies with lines similar to the lined paper students will use,

☆ plastic sheets in which you insert your lined transparencies,

☆ multicolored transparency pens.

If you don't have access to an overhead projector, you can model writing on chart paper or even on a chalk- or dry-erase board. (You'll still need pens or chalk in a variety of colors.) Bear in mind, though, that producing the model composition on a chalkboard or chart paper becomes increasingly cumbersome in grades 4–6, as the pieces are longer than those in previous grades and you will often work on the model over the course of several days.

Teachers should view model lessons in fourth through sixth grade as serving several purposes, all of which are important. Your lessons will

- ☆ model how writers get their ideas,

- ☆ model the basic conventions of writing,

- ☆ model good writing habits,

- ☆ model the writing process,

- ☆ offer writing options to students,

- ☆ give students the opportunity to apply other learning from other subject areas, and

- ☆ motivate students to write.

When a teacher uses a transparency to model writing, he or she can face the class and allow students to watch and listen to the decision-making and composing processes.

Thinking Aloud During the Mini-Lesson

Just as some students don't know how to actively reflect as they read, some students don't know how to think about writing as they're composing. Modeling the decisions that a writer must make, even the little ones, will allow those same thought processes to become part of your students' habits.

As important as modeling the composition itself is modeling the mental process involved in composing. A key component of modeling is "thinking aloud"—expressing aloud the decisions that writers must make as they write. For example, as you get started, you might say, "Oops! I surely can't start writing on this side of the page. I've got to turn my paper over so that I have the holes on the left side of the page to start. That's better! Okay, my name goes on the top line. I'll need to start over here on the left side to make sure my name fits in. I've got to look over at the calendar to check for today's date to write that on the next line. Now I'm ready to get started with my writing!"

If you haven't tried a Think Aloud with your students, it might seem a bit awkward at first. When aspects of writing are automatic for us as mature writers, it's sometimes difficult to slow down and think deliberately about what we're doing and why we're doing it. After practicing the Think Aloud for several days or weeks, you'll soon find that it gets much easier!

Establishing the Climate for Your Writing Workshop

At all grade levels, students need reassurance that no matter what their skill level, they will be accepted and encouraged as writers. Your most important responsibility, especially in the beginning of the year, is to create a safe environment in which risk taking is encouraged and students' early attempts are validated. As they realize that you will help them review or learn the basic tools necessary for good writing in a supportive classroom, they will be motivated to experiment with their writing.

We recommend starting your students' writing year slowly and informally. Ease yourself and your students into the habit of writing daily by writing about ordinary, everyday kinds of things. Let your students know that writing is just a basic communication skill. Take this opportunity to tell your students about yourself—your spouse, your children, your pets, your likes and dislikes, your memories, and whatever else will let them see that you have a life outside of school—since they rarely ever realize this!

Many teachers believe that their own model pieces should be extraordinary. This is erroneous, but more than that it is potentially harmful. Without realizing it, you might be discouraging students, who come away thinking, "I could never write about the things that my teacher knows." In our experience, we have found that we get students writing sooner when we write about ordinary things in our lives. In addition to helping them feel comfortable, writing about regular life is a way of teaching students that it isn't the topic that's critical—it's the way a writer transforms that topic. After all, the world's best writers write about ordinary events; through their special vision, the ordinary becomes the extraordinary.

Use the beginning of the year to read to them, too, from writers who will give them a glimpse of how the ordinary can be transformed. A book like Lois Lowry's *Looking Back: A Book of Memories*—a picture-book memoir in which she recounts experiences from her life that gave her the ideas for her award-winning books—can be a wonderful way to get your workshop going.

Here's another tip for getting going in the right direction at the beginning of the year: consider downplaying the more formal elements of planning for writing. We don't want to start off our students' writing year by flooding them with a string of exercises in brainstorming, graphic organizers, and conceptual maps. As the year progresses, we'll teach students all the tools they may need to write. But at the beginning, encourage students to simply have some fun flexing their "writing muscles," to ease back into writing by playing and experimenting with words on paper.

Our "keep it simple" approach to writing continues while we look daily for signs that students are developing confidence. What are the signs we're looking for? We observe their responses as we announce that it's time for the Writing Workshop—do they appear eager or reserved? We notice whether students are distracted during the mini-lesson or really attending to what we're writing. Do they seem to be picking up on the things we're modeling in our writing? When it's the students' turn to write, we look to see whether they are sitting hesitantly before putting pencils to paper or champing at the bit to set forth their new ideas. Afterward we observe whether they're all too happy to put their work away or excited to share their writing with others. Even the expression on their faces can provide a real clue!

When you see and hear these signs, it's time to move your workshop up a notch and incorporate the content units in this book.

> Sept. 6, 05
>
> Dear Students,
> I always enjoy reading You Are Special by Max Lucado. It reminds me of what it felt like when kids made fun of me for being too skinny, my long legs, and my glasses. It always hurt my feelings. I try to never put dots on other people. I hope you appreciate how very special you all are!
> Love,
> Mrs. Havens

By posting this informal letter to students about books they're reading, this teacher shares a simple model for students' own writing.

Beyond These Lessons

Most schools have approximately 180 days of instruction. This book offers instruction for about 63 days (59 lessons, some of which span two or more days). Even including the follow-up lesson ideas in the Quick Hints sections, a little quick math tells us that this isn't enough to fill up the school year. Rarely, however, would we expect a teacher to teach the concepts and skills included in this book only once! Even with the brightest of classes, the lessons need to be retaught and reinforced often.

With that said, we realize that you will need to create some of your own lessons as well. We've made that work easier for you by providing you with templates for them. Most of these mini-lessons offer you sample text (a content passage, example sentences, or brief story) to use in your initial teaching. In subsequent teachings just repeat the lesson using a sample text of your own to illustrate the same principle.

Remember, too, that you'll need to consult with your own curriculum guide to be sure that you're addressing all the standards and objectives required for your classroom. We advise that you put your curriculum guide side-by-side with our table of contents and check off the standards this book addresses. Then make note of the ones that aren't addressed. You'll want to fill in the gaps with your own lessons so that every standard or objective receives attention and direct instruction.

We sincerely hope that these mini-lessons help make the Writing Workshop a fun time of day for you and your students!

When your students are ready to launch into real writing in the Writing Workshop, the signs will be clear: They will be eager, attentive, and increasingly confident.

LANGUAGE ARTS STANDARDS INDEX*

STANDARDS BY PHASE	LESSON PAGE NUMBER
Planning for Writing	
Generate ideas for stories and descriptions in pictures and books, magazines, textbooks, the Internet, in conversation with others, and in newspapers, and through brainstorming	19, 20, 61, 84, 86, 91
Plan writing with details, using lists, graphic organizers, notes and logs, outlines, conceptual maps, learning logs, and timelines	23, 34, 52, 86, 87, 88, 90
Organize writing into a logical order: Select an organized structure/form that best suits purpose: chronological order, cause and effect, similarity and differences, pose and answer questions, climactic order, and general to specific; Choose a point of view based on purpose, audience, length and format requirements	23, 24, 32, 86, 109
Take notes from authoritative sources (i.e. almanacs, newspapers, periodicals, and the Internet) by identifying main ideas, evaluating relevancy, and paraphrasing information in resource materials	25, 34
Locate information by using prefaces, appendixes, citations, endnotes, and bibliographic references	20
Frame questions to direct research and raise new questions for further investigation	21
Writing the Draft	
Use resources for spelling: Use correct spelling for frequently used words (including irregular words, compound words, and homophones) and common word patterns	38, 103
Use basic computer skills for writing	101
Create and maintain a consistent voice to make writing interesting	18
Write effective beginning, middle, and end (including well-developed character, setting, and plot); Write drafts in an acceptable format	28, 30, 31
Write pieces with multiple paragraphs: Include an introductory paragraph with central idea and topic sentence; Include supporting paragraphs with appropriate facts, details, explanations, or concrete examples; Use appropriate transitions to link paragraphs; Write a concluding paragraph that summarizes points	32, 34, 87, 89, 109
Making Writing Cleaner and Clearer (Conventions)	
Nouns: Use regular and irregular plurals correctly	38
Verbs: Maintain consistency of tense, across paragraphs; Have verbs agree with compound subjects and with intervening phrases and clauses	39, 40
Pronouns: Use objective and subjective case pronouns; Have pronoun and antecedent agreement, including indefinite pronouns	41, 43
Adjectives: Use comparative and superlative forms of adjectives	44
Adverbs: Use adverb comparisons; Use adverbs correctly to make writing more precise	45, 65
Conjunctions: Use conjunctions to connect ideas and avoid excessive use	46
Prepositions: Use prepositional phrases to elaborate	47
Commas: Use commas with appositives; Use after introductory phrases and clauses	48, 49, 52
Quotation Marks: Use quotation marks in conversation, and in titles of articles, poems, songs, short stories, chapters, and documents	50
Apostrophes: Use apostrophes with singular and plural possessives	51
Colons and Semi-colons: Use colons to introduce a list; Use semi-colons to connect main clauses	52, 53
Capitalize appropriately: Capitalize a direct quote and proper nouns correctly	54
Write in complete sentences: Use a variety of sentence lengths and structures: simple, compound, complex with subordinate clauses and main clauses written correctly; Use a variety of sentence types (imperative, interrogative, exclamatory, declarative); Avoid fragments and run-ons	55, 56, 58

STANDARDS BY PHASE	LESSON PAGE NUMBER
Making Writing Better (Revision)	
Form imagery: Use figures of speech: similes, metaphors, analogies, alliteration, idioms, and symbolism; Use sensory details, and/or concrete examples	61, 63
Use transitions to connect ideas	24
Revise writing to improve word choice and precision of vocabulary; Choose strong verbs to make writing more vivid	64
Use adjectives and adverbs to make writing more vivid and/or precise	67
Make word choices appropriate to audience and purpose	61, 64, 69, 71, 73
Analyze published examples as models for writing	18
Create and maintain a consistent voice to make writing interesting	38, 103
Use resources for spelling: Use correct spelling for frequently used words (including irregular words, compound words, and homophones) and common word patterns; Use classroom resources for spelling (dictionary, thesaurus, spell checker)	101
Use basic computer skills for writing	72, 73, 74
Revise writing for meaning, clarity, and focus: Add and delete; Combine and rearrange words, sentences, and paragraphs; Use modifiers, coordination, and subordination to expand and embed ideas	30, 71, 109
Writing in a Variety of Forms	
Write narratives that describe and explain familiar objects, events, and experiences: Use a range of narrative devices, i.e. dialogue or suspense; Use literary conflict, elements, and devices	28, 30, 31
Write in response to what is read and written	78, 86
Write informational pieces, summarizing and organizing ideas gained from multiple sources in useful ways, including charts, graphs, outlines, and lists	25, 32, 34, 87, 88, 109
Write summaries of reading selections to include main ideas and significant details	82, 95
Write a friendly letter	84
Write persuasive pieces: Support with relevant evidence and effective emotional appeals; Follow simple organizational pattern with most appealing statements first, address reader concerns; Write persuasive pieces for different purposes (for example, pieces about events, books, issues, experiences, letters, including letters to the editor)	86
Write class newsletter articles	90, 91
Write patterned, rhymed, unrhymed, and free verse poems	73, 93, 94
Write in learning logs and journals to discover, develop and refine ideas, including other curricular areas	95
Use the Internet to communicate with family and friends	96
Write plays, scripts, and other productions	97
Polishing and Publishing Our Writing	
Edit for correctness, meaning, and clarity: Use appropriate references when editing—including dictionary, books, and simple thesaurus	103, 104, 107
Use a simple checklist for revising and editing, working independently and collaboratively	101, 104
Use organizational features of printed text (page numbering, alphabetizing, glossaries, chapter heading, tables of contents, indexes, and captions)	105
Respond in constructive ways to others' writings	94, 104, 106, 107
Share writing orally with others	80, 94, 97, 106, 107
Publish in various formats	78, 80, 109
Review own writing to set goals for growth	107, 108

* Along with the National Standards, the standards of the following ten states were gathered to create the curriculum for this book: California, Colorado, Florida, Indiana, New York, Pennsylvania, South Carolina, Texas, Virginia, and Washington.

Planning for Writing

Especially as the school year begins, students should have the opportunity to build their confidence in writing slowly but surely. Keep in mind that there may be several obstacles you'll have to help them overcome during the first several weeks. Some students may not have had ample writing opportunities during the preceding school years. Even students who wrote frequently in previous grades may have become rusty and out of practice during summer vacation. For one reason or another, almost all of your students may need some time to get the hang of writing regularly. Plan to take it slow and easy.

For these reasons, we recommend concentrating on writing as merely a basic communication skill at the start of the school year. Encourage students to "talk on paper" so that they become fluent and confident in their written communication. To begin, we suggest using lessons like the first one in this section. In this lesson students are encouraged to spend classroom time writing notes to their classmates. This is a simple, fun way of telling students that writing is talking on paper, plain and simple. Next, encourage students to write about ordinary everyday experiences in a conversational way. This is an intentional strategy to set students at ease, especially those who don't readily accept that they are writers.

In typical informal conversation, speakers don't stop to map out words or make a written list of the things they might talk about before the words roll off their tongue. Writing in the beginning of the year should be handled the same way. Hold off using graphic and other formal, conceptual organizers for a few weeks, as students tend to view these devices as just more hoops they have to jump through. Your message should be that mental drafting is allowed, even preferred.

Once students possess confidence in themselves as writers, they're ready to begin to experiment with styles and types of writing. Especially as their writing grows in complexity, one way that we'll want to stretch them is to expose them to different ways of generating ideas and planning how to write about them. To help students plan writing, we'll want to give them a whole menu of tools from which they can pick and choose based on their preferences or on the type of writing. In this section, we'll explore

☆ visual prompts and informational book elements as springboards for generating ideas for writing,

☆ question-framing procedures for planning and organizing writing,

☆ graphic organizers and conceptual maps for planning writing,

☆ text patterns to aid in organizing writing,

☆ note-taking methods that help focus a piece of writing.

A number of these activities help students form mental images. As the work of Gambrell and Koskinen (2002) has shown, a visual framework for organizing information helps learners comprehend, remember, and integrate information across texts.

Additionally, we suggest that you consult your own state's standards to check whether they require students to use particular methods for performance-based writing tests. If, for instance, you find that there is a graphic organizer highlighted in your testing program, you will want to use it with greater frequency in your modeling. However, even in this case we would not recommend limiting your modeling exclusively to that organizer. As mentioned earlier, we need to give our young writers a wide range of tools to choose from, including graphic organizers, semantic maps, story maps, brainstorming, lists, and outlining. Through observing your daily modeling and then experimenting with different methods, each student (just like more practiced writers) will decide what works best for him or her.

Some teachers and students mistakenly view the preliminaries of writing—the focus of this section—as laborious and unnecessary. We hope you come to see that, on the contrary, the planning stages are an exciting launch point for all the real writing that is to come. By providing students with many choices, we are helping them to personalize their planning. And when planning is personalized, the writing is more likely to be "just right" as well!

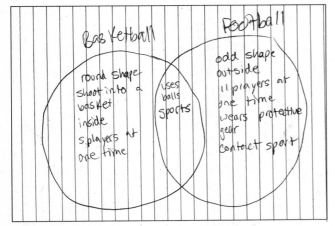

This student has used a Venn diagram to organize his thoughts as he plans to write about different sports.

This student's thoughtful categorizing of three different senses, each of which becomes a different detail paragraph, results in a well-organized essay.

Linking speaking to writing

Skill Focus

Transferring speaking voice to writing; creating and maintaining a consistent voice to make writing interesting

Materials & Resources

☆ Scrap paper for note writing

☆ Timer

Quick Hints

As follow-up to this lesson, the next time you have an interruption to your class and need to keep your students "busy" for a few minutes, give them permission to talk on paper rather than out loud.

STEPS

1. Tell students that the writing lesson today is a little unusual: They can just "talk." There's one catch, however—everything they say to their friends must be written rather than spoken. In other words, they have permission, for a change, to write notes to each other!

2. Establish these basic rules before getting started:

   ☆ No talking out loud.

   ☆ No sitting idly—you must always be writing. If you pass a note to someone and you're waiting for them to write back, you need to start another conversation with someone else.

   ☆ Include everyone! If you notice classmates who aren't writing, write them a quick note to keep them busy. Use the activity as an opportunity to get to know students you don't know well.

3. Distribute scrap paper to students, set a timer for 10–15 minutes, and see what happens! No doubt your students will have fun "talking" on paper.

4. Model keeping busy writing yourself. Gather your own scrap paper and pull a desk up alongside groups of students. Write fast and furiously to keep as many students engaged in conversation as possible.

5. After the timer goes off, hold a class discussion related to the activity students have just engaged in. Guide the discussion to include the following important points:

   ☆ Writing is just a basic communication skill. Even if students don't grow up to become renowned authors, they will all be expected to communicate clearly and powerfully in the workplace.

   ☆ Writing doesn't always require a great deal of planning.

   ☆ Informal note writing, such as students have just experienced, often involves a great deal of personality, or "writer's voice." Many people feel most comfortable just talking on paper and tend to use their own "everyday language" and expressions in personal notes.

6. Have students examine their own notes. Ask them to list aspects and characteristics of these notes that might be different from the type of more formal writing they have done in the past. Challenge them to consider this question: How can you preserve that voice and transfer its liveliness or other appealing qualities to your other writing?

Generating ideas for writing

EXPLANATION: When students are asked to write about a self-selected topic, many spend too much time just deciding on a topic. Skillful teachers can help students home in on topics through prewriting activities such as group brainstorming (Zemelman, Daniels & Hyde, 1998). In this prewriting lesson students apply these methods to visual materials in order to generate ideas for writing.

Skill Focus

Generating ideas for stories and descriptions by using visual images to stimulate conversation and brainstorming

Materials & Resources

☆ Magazines, old textbooks, photos, postcards, newspapers, catalogs, and the Internet (for clip art and other images)

☆ Transparency sleeves

☆ Index cards

☆ Paper clips and scissors

Quick Hints

Students garner so many ideas for writing from one another. Invite each small group to choose a favorite picture and share it with the other groups. Display these selected pictures on a bulletin board; enhance the display by encircling it with tiny clear lights.

STEPS

1. Tell students that today they will use visual materials to help them come up with ideas for writing. Explain that first you will demonstrate how you do this yourself as the inspiration for writing an original piece.

2. For example, display a photo, cut from a magazine, of a small boy and his dog peering over a brick wall. Model how you brainstorm ways this photo stimulates your imagination. You might say something like the following:

   This picture makes me wonder what the boy sees beyond the wall— it could be so many different things, a field of tall cornstalks baking in the sun, a graveyard for old abandoned cars and trucks, or a rocky coastline eroded by ocean waves are just three things I think of. So I could choose one of these to write about.

   Alternately, or in addition, you could show a photo of a beautiful castle cut from an old social studies textbook, brainstorming aloud this way:

   This castle reminds me of the medieval times, when knights and kings ruled the land. Wow! A story with this castle as the setting would be fun to write.

3. After modeling these ideas verbally, write each one on an index card and paper-clip it to the appropriate picture.

4. Divide the class into groups of three or four students. Provide the groups with old textbooks, magazines, and the like and have each student select and cut out personally intriguing pictures. Encourage group brainstorming to generate ideas for writing based on the pictures. Have each student record the ideas relating to his or her selected photos on index cards.

5. Finally, provide each student with a three-hole-punched clear transparency sleeve with a top opening to store his or her pictures and paper-clipped ideas. When students are searching at a later date for an idea to write about, encourage them to look through their stored pictures and cards.

Locating information for writing

EXPLANATION: In this lesson students are exposed to another helpful means of finding a topic for writing— browsing reference materials for subjects that interest them. There are three prongs to this lesson: students review reference book aids, such as appendixes; they learn to think of these aids as sources for writing ideas; and they gain experience reading and interpreting a time line.

Skill Focus

Locating information by using prefaces, appendixes, citations, endnotes, and bibliographic references; generating ideas for writing; reading and interpreting a time line

Materials & Resources

☆ Reference books with appendixes

Quick Hints

Generate further interest and motivation about writing by creating a hallway or bulletin board display of the student quick-write reports created in this lesson. Use the time line itself as the framework for the display and position each report in its appropriate slot along the time line.

STEPS

1. Tell students that in this lesson they'll learn a way to generate ideas for writing nonfiction pieces such as social studies reports. Remind students that reference books usually include aids such as endnotes, bibliographies, and appendixes. Explain that not only can students use these items in ways that are familiar— as reading and study aids—but they can also turn to them as sources for ideas for writing.

2. Share with students that you'll highlight one particular informational resource in this lesson—an appendix containing a historical time line. Below is an example of a time line for the 1970s:

   1970 The Beatles break up as a group and decide to perform individually.

   1971 Cigarette advertising is banned on TV and radio.

   1972 Pong starts the videogame craze.

   1973 Vice President Spiro Agnew resigns as a result of income tax evasion.

   1974 The U.S. and the Soviets meet in space.

   1975 Microsoft is founded.

   1976 Jimmy Carter is elected to serve as 39th president of the United States.

   1977 Elvis Presley dies at 42 years of age.

   1978 John Paul II becomes Pope.

   1979 Susan B. Anthony, an activist for the cause of women's suffrage, is commemorated on a U.S. coin, the Susan B. Anthony dollar.

3. Read this list aloud and model how you brainstorm to decide on a topic that interests you. As you select one—say, the U.S. and the Soviets meeting in space—think aloud to show students the decision-making thought process involved. For instance, elaborate on the connections it sparks, personal interests it taps, learning goals it addresses, and so on.

4. Next, organize students into small groups. Have the groups discuss events from the time line, following your modeled decision making, and select a topic to write about. Bring the groups together to share their selections and the reasoning behind their selections.

5. Following the discussion, have each student do a quick write about the topic their group chose. (A quick write is a procedure in which a writer jots down thoughts as they come to mind in a brief period of time.)

6. Conclude by stressing that the time line is only one of a vast number of resources that students can use for homing in on ideas for writing. Invite students to suggest additional informational appendixes and other book elements they might use.

Framing questions to direct research

EXPLANATION: Particularly at the intermediate grades, we want to nurture the natural curiosity that students possess about the world around them. If students are guided in their research gathering and reporting by their passion for and curiosity about the topic, their writing is likely to be not only of a higher quality but also more enjoyable for them to do. The goal for this lesson is to give students practice brainstorming and forming questions that can be the basis for their research and information writing. Eventually they may write a composition based on the specific questions posed here, but even if they do not, the question-framing process is invaluable.

Skill Focus

Framing questions to direct research and writing

Materials & Resources

☆ Several sheets of unlined paper, each cut into as large a circle as possible. (See Preliminary Considerations for further information.)

Quick Hints

Direct students to the Wonder Wheel Wall or Mobiles when they are stumped for a writing topic. Invite them to browse through the topics and questions that might inspire their writing.

Preliminary Considerations: *For this lesson, you'll create a Wonder Wheel Wall (a wall filled with wheels of questions about particular topics) or a set of Wonder Wheel Mobiles (three to four wheels of questions hung from a coat hanger with string) for your classroom. (See diagram at the end of the lesson for an example.) You can approach this lesson several different ways, depending on your own students' needs and abilities. You might choose to model creating the wheels while students watch and subsequently create their own; you might create model wheels and invite students to work right along with you, creating their own simultaneously; or you might create the wheels yourself but with ongoing input from the students. If you choose either of the first options, each student will need a set of materials.*

STEPS

1. For each Wonder Wheel: Fold the circle in half three times according to the diagram. Unfold the paper, which should now have eight equal sections. Using a topic that your class has recently studied or will soon study, write the general topic in the middle of the circle where all of the "spokes" converge.

2. Model how you brainstorm eight questions that pique your curiosity about the topic. Write each question in one of the sections of the wheel until the eight sections are filled.

3. Think aloud about the questions and decide which three would be especially good for guiding further research. Consider such criteria as the following:

   Characteristics of Questions That Work Best
   - They are thought-provoking, interesting questions about which you and others may be curious.
   - They aren't too broad—they help you pinpoint specific information easily.
   - They aren't too narrow—also so they can help you pinpoint specific information easily.
   - They are directly related to the topic.

4. Turn the circle over and trace the folds with your pencil to form four equal parts, rather than the original eight. Transfer the three questions you've selected to three of the sections. In the remaining section of the circle, think aloud to frame a main idea statement that will be the basis of your paper. Write it in a different color from the three questions. (See examples below.)

5. Display the Wonder Wheels as described in Preliminary Considerations.

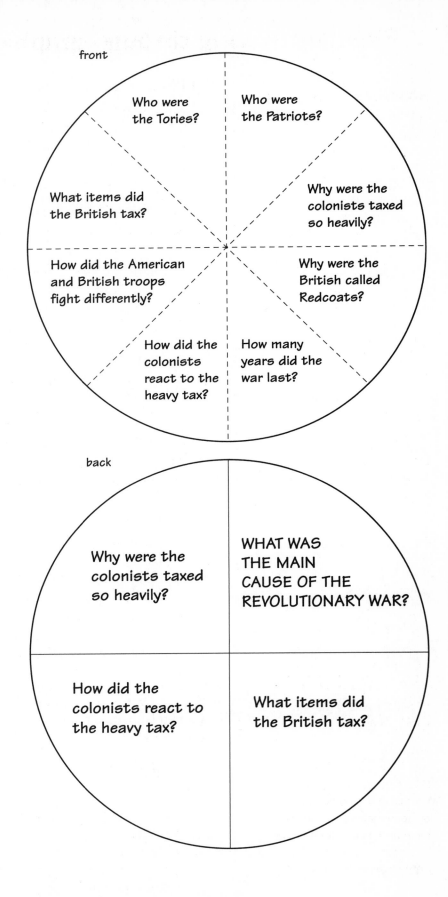

front

Who were
the Tories?

Who were
the Patriots?

What items did
the British tax?

Why were the
colonists taxed
so heavily?

How did the American
and British troops
fight differently?

Why were the
British called
Redcoats?

How did the
colonists
react to the
heavy tax?

How many
years did the
war last?

back

Why were the
colonists taxed
so heavily?

WHAT WAS
THE MAIN
CAUSE OF THE
REVOLUTIONARY WAR?

How did the
colonists react to
the heavy tax?

What items did
the British tax?

Planning writing through graphic conceptualizing

EXPLANATION: By the intermediate grades, most students have had a good deal of experience using various graphic organizers to plan their writing. This lesson helps prepare students for more independence in their planning. After you guide them to conceptualize visually the organization and purpose of their writing, they work in groups to make key decisions about selecting appropriate organizers.

Skill Focus

Planning writing with graphic organizers and conceptual maps; selecting an organized structure or form that best suits writing purpose

Materials & Resources

☆ Transparency of selected graphic organizers

Quick Hints

Provide further practice for students to visually conceptualize and organize their writing by challenging them to come up with creative graphic organizers. Occasionally provide students with a description of a writing piece that is in the planning stages and have them create an original organizer for this composition. Display these organizers in your classroom so that other students may experiment with them.

STEPS

1. Review with students that organization is an important element in planning a piece of writing. Review as well that the best way to organize for a particular composition depends on the nature and purpose of that piece. Thoughtful writers consider their goals and then select an appropriate organizational plan.

2. Draw these basic organizers on a transparency or on the chalkboard:

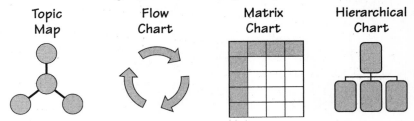

Topic Map   Flow Chart   Matrix Chart   Hierarchical Chart

3. Tell students that you are planning to write a certain composition. You might describe it this way: "I want to write a piece that compares the habitats of animals in different environments."

4. Model for students how you select the most appropriate organizer for this composition. You might think aloud as follows:

    Comparisons usually require putting two or more things side-by-side to see how they are alike and different. Some of these organizers imply sequence, which isn't the objective of comparing habitats. Some show equally important details. Some show a hierarchy of what's more and less important—which, again, isn't the reason for my writing. I need to choose an organizer that helps me compare several animals and habitats. The Matrix Chart allows me to write the names of various animals down or across the outside row or column and the characteristics of the habitat, so this is my choice.

5. Organize students into small groups and describe your plans for several new compositions. Challenge each group to choose the organizer that would be most logical for planning each composition. Tell them to be ready to defend their choice as well as to explain why they would not choose the other graphics. Following are several sample planning statements you might use:

    "I want to write about the different branches of the United States government and the responsibilities of each of those branches."

    "I want to write about the process of purifying water in a city sanitation system."

    "I want to write about the distinguishing characteristics of the state of New York."

6. Have each group report back to the class to discuss the decision they've made and their justifications for choosing one organizer and not choosing others.

Organizing writing in a logical order

EXPLANATION: In this lesson students are exposed to material that is organized in a particular text pattern—cause and effect. When passages are organized in a logical pattern (whether it be chronological order, compare and contrast, question and answer, or cause and effect), they can help readers develop new understandings through forming a network of connections (Zemelman, Daniels & Hyde, 1998). After you model and discuss this pattern, students should find it much easier to transfer this kind of organization to their own writing.

Skill Focus

Organizing writing in a logical order; selecting an organizing structure or form that best suits purpose (cause and effect)

Materials & Resources

☆ Textbook passages, the Internet, newspapers

Quick Hints

As a prewriting activity, ask students to search for cause-and-effect statements in newspaper articles. Have students work individually, in pairs, or in small groups to highlight examples and then share their examples with the class.

STEPS

1. Review with students that what and how they read can help them in their own writing. Tell them that in this lesson they will have the opportunity to examine informational material that is organized in a cause-and-effect text pattern. By learning to identify the causes and the effects in this reading material, they will be gaining knowledge about how to organize their own writing.

2. Using a transparency, poster board, or the chalkboard, display preselected passages from social studies materials or cause-and-effect statements you have generated yourself. For example, you might use the samples below (the correct identification for each statement is provided for your convenience):

   After the Revolutionary War, Americans believed that they had rights to all the land on the continent. Many settlers moved into Texas, which was owned by Mexico. After defeating the Mexicans (**cause**), Sam Houston declared Texas an independent republic (**effect**).

   The United States and Mexico went to war over borders in 1846 (**cause**). The U.S. won the war by conquering Mexican forces in New Mexico, California, and Mexico City. Under the terms of the peace treaty the U.S. bought CA, NV, UT, AZ, NM, CO, and WY from Mexico (**effect**).

   Also during this growth period of the United States, pioneers chose to settle in the Oregon country (**cause**). Thousands of these travelers used the route known as the Oregon Trail to go westward (**effect**).

   About the same time, gold was discovered in California (**cause**). In 1849 more than 80,000 gold seekers followed the Oregon Trail and then went south to California (**effect**).

3. Read these statements aloud to the class and model for students the text organization pattern by identifying which parts of the sentences are causes and which parts are effects. You may rewrite the sentences to illustrate the cause and effect elements, underline them, or distinguish them in another way to help students identify the parts. For example:

   After defeating the Mexicans (**cause**),

   Sam Houston declared Texas an independent republic (**effect**).

4. Now have students select one set of facts and do some research in their textbooks or other resources to add new details to the information. For example, they might read further about the attack on the Alamo or the origins of the Oregon Trail.

5. Finally, ask students to use these new details to create a new, brief passage. Challenge them to include at least two cause-and-effect sentences within their new paragraph.

Taking note of it

STEPS

Skill Focus

Taking notes from authoritative sources by identifying main ideas; evaluating relevance; paraphrasing information in resource materials

Materials & Resources

☆ Short informational text such as a social studies or science textbook excerpt or a reading from the Internet

Quick Hints

Try this "big picture" challenge in all the different content areas. It's a good way to help students avoid getting entangled in interesting details that sometimes obscure the big picture.

1. Share the following basic rules of note taking with your students. You might write these on a transparency or on poster board to display as a classroom chart.

   - Look or listen for the "big picture" ideas. Hint: In text and in oral presentations, these are usually at the beginning and the end.
   - Look or listen for key words that are emphasized. Try to make a connection between these and the big picture. Hint: Take special note of words that are repeated often.
   - Use text signal words to help guide you. Hint: Words and phrases such as *most important, in conclusion,* and *remember that* often introduce big ideas.
   - Find the fewest words possible to capture meaning and use these essential words for your note taking. Hint: Every *a, an,* and *the* can't be important!

2. Display a short text—a book page or a lengthy paragraph—and read it aloud. After reading, model for students how you take notes based on this material. Tell the class that you have a challenge: You must jot down no more than 20 words. If you wind up with more than 20 words on your first pass, demonstrate how you can strike excess words and sum up ideas more concisely to meet the length requirement. This will help students understand the process of refining their original notes. To engage them more actively, you may ask for their suggestions as you do the pruning.

3. Write an original short summary based on the words, concepts, and ideas represented in your 20-word list. For example, using an excerpt from www.enchantedlearning.com on the subject of inventors, here is a sample 20-word set of notes and summary:

   Notes:
   First aerosol spray can
   1944 Lyle Goodloe, W.N. Sullivan – U.S. inventors
   Kill malaria carrying mosquitoes for World War II soldiers

   Summary:
   The first aerosol spray can was invented in the U.S. by Lyle Goodloe and W.N. Sullivan in an attempt to enable soldiers to spray and kill malaria-carrying mosquitoes overseas during World War II.

4. Finally, provide students with a different selection to read. Organize them into cooperative groups. Challenge the groups to use no more than 20 words to capture the key words and ideas and then to write a short summary of the passage. (Be sure that students realize that the 20-word limit is an arbitrary number you've set for this assignment; what's important is that they learn to use a minimal number of words to capture meaning while note taking.)

Writing the Draft

The actual writing—putting the pencil to paper—is usually the most difficult time for students during the Writing Workshop, at least in the beginning. Most students quickly learn to enjoy brainstorming for ideas and planning for writing. But pulling it all together is far more challenging. There's so much to think about at the same time: *What's the most appropriate title? Do I need to indent here? What's a good topic sentence? Do I have enough details in this paragraph? Am I remembering all of the story elements? Have I created a setting that makes sense?* And this is just a sampling of the questions facing young writers. It's a tough job, indeed, for students to synthesize all they've learned and to communicate their creative thoughts at the same time.

As their classroom teacher and writing coach, you can make draft writing easier for them by implementing the following five guidelines:

1. Continue to reassure students that you want them to get their thoughts on paper regardless of the correctness of their writing. The only requirement related to correctness is that students observe the Quick Check list (see Section Three introduction, page 36) at the end of their daily writing. That shouldn't be a tedious exercise; it should become a habit. Students should understand that the Quick Check is done so that the next time they return to their writing, it'll be much easier to reconnect to their thoughts because the draft will be cleaner and clearer to work with. Also, if they share this draft as a potential publishing piece, it'll be much easier for you (or a peer) to read it and give feedback. Your reassurance that you're not looking for a perfect paper will help your young writers become more fluent.

2. Remind students that they can take as long as they need to write a piece in the Writing Workshop. With some exceptions, they do not have to meet an end-of-class deadline. It's permissible, even encouraged, to work on a piece for a few days, a week, or longer in the Writing Workshop. Untimed writing tends to relieve the pressure of writer's block.

3. Create a classroom atmosphere that is conducive to writing. If you treat the Writing Workshop like "office time," where students understand that their daily job is to generate writing, they may be more focused and serious about the work they're expected to generate each day. If you feel

comfortable accommodating students' suggestions and preferences, elicit their input about what would help them become productive writers. After a discussion, you might make a list of agreed-upon points and display it in the classroom. Here are some points that students might bring up:

☆ Rearrange desks so that students' privacy is ensured.

☆ Allow them to lie on the floor or sit on bean bag chairs while they write in their notebooks.

☆ Have them write inside "carrels" created by propping opened file folders on their desks.

☆ Include time daily for optional peer meetings to share ideas about writing.

Whenever the Writing Workshop isn't running smoothly, stop and review what the students agreed upon as their working conditions to find out what's not working and why.

4. Expose students regularly to as many samples of writing as possible in a multitude of genres and styles. To be good writers, students need to read a great deal and look at the text through the eyes of a writer. Your daily mini-lessons will allow them to see and hear your writing and sometimes the writing of published authors. And if you build in time at the end of each day's workshop for students to share their work with one another, you'll also expose them to a further source of inspiration: their peers' work. All of these samples become part of students' writing background and can help them to develop into better writers.

5. Finally, offer students praise and encouragement. The praise you offer should be genuine, however. If a student's writing isn't truly well developed, don't say that it is. Students must learn to evaluate their own writing efforts. The criteria you use for what is their "good," "better," and "best" writing will quickly set their own personal standards. There's always something genuinely good that can be said about a student's work. Perhaps the writer whose work is not yet well developed put in a great deal of effort or chose a particularly intriguing concept to write about. Applaud these aspects. Keep them motivated!

As you establish a writing classroom based on these guidelines, we believe you'll discover how smoothly lessons and instruction will flow. This section provides you with four lessons to help you launch your students into the drafting phase. The first three lessons focus on story writing, emphasizing different angles of narratives—including work with story elements (especially plot and character) and story structure (introduction, rising action, climax, resolution, and reflection). The final lesson, which has two parts and should span multiple days, highlights expository writing. It offers students a helpful graphic to organize their informational writing and a model for turning these organizers into compositions. This kind of writing is especially valuable in the intermediate grades as students' learning within the content areas becomes increasingly important.

Students enjoy the opportunity to write in informal spots around the classroom and to confer with their peers.

Writing an effective story: focus on plot

EXPLANATION: A well-developed story requires an effective beginning, middle, and end. By the time students reach the intermediate grades, they have heard many stories read aloud and have read stories independently, as well. They should start this lesson, therefore, with a good working sense of this basic story structure. Today's lesson helps them review story structure and then challenges them to write a new draft of a story, with a focus on one particular plot component.

Skill Focus

Identifying basic story elements of setting, character, and plot; identifying and writing an effective beginning, middle, and end for a story

Materials & Resources

☆ A simple narrative story or book for reading aloud (used in this lesson: *Arthur's Teacher Moves In* by Marc Brown)

☆ Story map (see Appendix, page 113)

Quick Hints

Invite students to illustrate their individual Arthur stories. Bind all the stories into a class book. Students will enjoy comparing the various plots created by their classmates.

STEPS

1. Review with students the three essential elements of a narrative story: setting (including time and place), character, and plot. Tell them that today's lesson will focus on plot and especially on the three segments that form the framework of narrative stories: beginning, middle, and end.

2. Read aloud a story with a very simple plot line, such as *Arthur's Teacher Moves In* by Marc Brown. A simple story is best for this lesson because it makes it easier for students to identify the various story elements and the plot segments.

3. Using a transparency of a story map, fill in the story elements and the plot segments for this story. See below for a completed sample story map.

Name _____		Date _____
A STORY MAP		
Selection: *Arthur's Teacher Moves In*		
SETTING		
Place:	Arthur's house, the school	
Time:	the present	
CHARACTERS	Arthur Arthur's family Mr. Ratburn, Arthur's teacher Classmates	
PLOT/EVENTS		
Beginning:	Mr. Ratburn's roof caves in from heavy snow and he moves in with Arthur's family.	
Middle:	Arthur tries to act smarter than he is. Arthur is not happy about the teacher living with him. Mr. Ratburn wins Arthur over by performing magic tricks, watching funny videos, dressing casually, etc. Arthur gets an "A" on a test. His classmates think he is receiving special treatment. His classmates turn against him.	
End:	Mr. Ratburn decides to move in with some of the other children to take some of the heat off Arthur.	

4. After the story map is complete, engage the class in a discussion to analyze the plot further. Ask questions like these to encourage students to examine each of the events: How can you tell where the plot shifts from the beginning to the middle to the end? Does one

event seem to lead naturally to another or are there unexpected plot twists? Where is the action most exciting? Did you feel the end resolved the tension in the story in a way that made sense?

5. Challenge students to rewrite this story, creating a more elaborate version based on the story map information. Assign certain students (or small groups) a specific plot segment. Some students will rewrite the beginning, others will create a new middle, and still others will create a new end. Before students begin writing, brainstorm different situations or scenarios for each plot segment. For instance, for a new middle, here are two situations that could prove intriguing:

- A conversation at the dinner table in which the teacher reports that Arthur has misbehaved at school.
- The teacher tells Arthur's sister, D.W., that Arthur has a girlfriend.

Using literary conflict and elements in writing a story

Skill Focus

Identifying basic story elements of setting, character, and plot; using literary elements to describe and explain experiences

Materials & Resources

☆ Familiar story, such as a fairy tale (used in this lesson: "Cinderella")

Quick Hints

Make available excellent examples of books that have climactic plot elements. Invite students to select one of the books and to map out the events of the plot using the roller-coaster diagram.

STEPS

1. Review with students the story structure of beginning, middle, and end. Then, on a transparency or the chalkboard, write the following terms and discuss how they match up with and correspond to the beginning, middle, and end structure.
   * Introduction
   * Rising Action
   * Climax
   * Resolution
   * Ending/Reflection

2. Tell students that these terms are sometimes called "climactic plot elements"; they take readers on a journey that is much like a ride on a roller coaster. To help students better visualize this, draw the following chart on a transparency or the board:

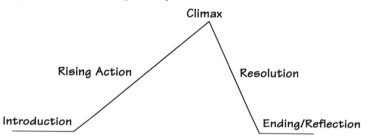

3. With the class, use the above diagram to chart the actions of a character. You might use a familiar fairy tale or folk tale to help students better grasp the concepts. Below is a sample completed diagram based on "Cinderella":

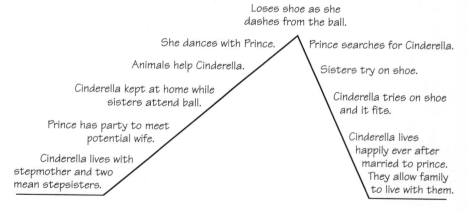

4. Challenge students (either individually or in small groups) to map out the action of a folk tale or fairy tale. Be sure they use the specific terms you have taught, as well as the roller-coaster diagram for the mapping. If time permits (or on a subsequent day), have students use their maps to flesh out and draft original stories.

Writing an effective story: focus on character

EXPLANATION: This lesson examines character development by focusing on a classic short story, Jack London's "To Build a Fire." By exploring a character's thoughts, feelings, and conflicts, readers can understand the significance of the story's events. Ralph Fletcher and Joann Portalupi (1998), suggest that to cause the reader to care for a character, the writer must provide a sense of the character's inner life. Our goal here is to guide students to apply what they learn from their reading to their own writing.

Skill Focus

Identifying story elements; analyzing and employing character development; using literary conflict and elements

Materials & Resources

☆ "To Build a Fire" by Jack London

☆ Transparencies

Quick Hints

Invite students to brainstorm a character's internal and external traits using a heart-shaped map. Outside the rim of the heart, students write words that describe the character's appearance, such as *rugged, stubbly beard.* Inside the heart, students write words that describe the character's feelings and temperament, such as *confident, egotistical.*

Note: *We recommend that you preview Jack London's "To Build a Fire" (often included in anthologies) to determine whether it is appropriate for your students' reading level or whether this is a story you'll need to share as a class Read Aloud. Before the start of the lesson, be sure all students have either read or heard the story.*

STEPS

1. Tell students that this lesson will help them understand how writers develop characters in narrative writing. A story's main characters' personalities (what they think, feel, and believe) affect the action of the story. At the same time, the conflict that the author has set up in the plot affects how the characters act. So there is an important back-and-forth movement between and among story elements. Good readers watch out for this to help them better understand the story.

2. Call students' attention to Jack London's own analysis of his main character. On a transparency or the chalkboard, write the following key lines from "To Build a Fire": "The trouble with him was that he was without imagination. He was quick and alert in the things of life, but only in the things, and not in the significances."

3. Hold a class discussion to brainstorm what the author means by the statement above. Ask students, in what ways was the character often quite alert about things but at the same time unaware of their significance? Guide students to focus on how the author used the element of conflict to convey the personality of the character.

4. In tandem with the discussion, help students make lists of the things the character was aware of and their unrecognized significance. You might create a T-chart with headings, such as that shown below:

Alert about these things	Significance
He knew it was probably colder than 50 degrees below zero.	He didn't consider the worst that could possibly happen.
The old-timer told him not to be out alone at 50 degrees below.	He didn't think anything could happen to him—he could keep his head.
He was aware that there were hidden springs.	He thought being aware would keep him safe.
He knew nature was capable of killing.	He thought he could outsmart nature.

5. Finally, invite students to create their own short stories, employing the skills and knowledge they have gained from this lesson about character and the previous two lessons about plot and climax. They should first map out and then draft a story that involves a conflict in which a main character faces a crisis that reveals both the limits and the strengths of his personality. Note that the stories do not have to be serious; like the Arthur story, they can be humorous. The goal is to focus on character development.

Two-Part Lesson: Writing a Multiple-Paragraph Composition
Part 1: **Planning the paragraphs**

EXPLANATION: In the intermediate grades, students are expected to know how to write both narrative stories (as discussed in the previous three lessons) and informational compositions. These nonfiction pieces are increasingly sophisticated, usually involving multiple paragraphs. Some students (and some adults!) are overwhelmed by the thought of managing that much text. This two-part lesson demonstrates that writing and organizing longer text is easier if you think about it in "chunks" and if you understand the purpose of each "chunk." This first part focuses on planning the piece.

Skill Focus

Writing informational pieces with multiple paragraphs

Materials & Resources

☆ Transparency, prepared ahead, of a camera graphic organizer (see Appendix, page 114)

☆ Photocopies, one for each student, of the organizer

Quick Hints

Occasionally ask students to use the camera graphic to demonstrate their understanding of the big-picture idea and several supporting ideas in content lessons they're studying.

STEPS

1. Tell students that in this two-part lesson they are going to practice planning for and then composing a multiple-paragraph informational essay. Because the process of planning for a multiple-paragraph composition can be equally as important as actually writing the piece, today's lesson will focus only on this first step.

2. Share with students that writing multiple-paragraph pieces can be quite simple if they understand what's being accomplished by each part of the text. Present and discuss this basic framework for a five-paragraph nonfiction piece:

   - **First paragraph:** *The writer needs to present the overall idea or the big picture. The writer asks: What's the main idea I want my readers to know? This becomes paragraph 1.*

   - **Middle portion of the piece:** *Writers generally like to have at least three ideas that support or illustrate the big picture. Each idea becomes a different paragraph, in this case paragraphs 2, 3, and 4.*

   - **Conclusion to the piece:** *The writer comes full circle and emphasizes the big picture again, using a different presentation of the idea. This becomes paragraph 5.*

3. To help students better visualize this framework, we suggest presenting a prepared transparency of a camera graphic organizer (see the end of this lesson for a completed sample graphic and Appendix, page 114 for a blank template). In this organizer, the top camera represents the main idea; the frames of film stand for the three ideas that support the main point; and the final image, a repeat of the top camera, represents the conclusion, thereby showing how it connects back to the main idea.

4. After displaying a transparency of the blank template for the class, model how you use it to plan out an informational composition you intend to write. The completed sample below, for an essay titled "How Animals Adapt to Their Ecosystems," demonstrates one possible plan.

5. Distribute photocopies of the camera graphic. Have students work individually or in small groups to choose their own informational topic and to fill in the camera planner, following the model you have provided. (Note: This step may require an additional day or two, as students will need to do some research on their topic in order to generate their main ideas and supporting details.)

Animals adapt
to their
ecosystems in
many interesting
ways.

Body coverings of different kinds are key to survival.	Feet, toes, and talons protect on land, air, and water.	Body and head shapes protect animals.

The degree to
which animals
adapt to their
ecosystems is
quite amazing!

Sample Five-Paragraph Composition Based on the Organizer, (See Part 2, Step 3)

How Animals Adapt to Their Ecosystems

Animals adapt to their ecosystems in many interesting ways. These adaptations allow the animals to survive in specific habitats. Animal body features provide the needed protection.

Body coverings of different kinds are the key to survival. The scales of a reptile protect it from injury and prevent drying in the hot desert sun. The fur that covers a bison keeps the animal warm in the winter, but that same fur may be shed for cooling in the summer.

Feet, toes, and talons protect animals on land, in the air, and in water. Birds' talons, which allow them to swiftly capture a mouse for food, can be tucked under their body when a speedy exit is needed. A penguin's feet are shaped for accurate steering during swimming. The two-toed feet of an ostrich enable this bird to run on land.

Body and head shapes protect animals. The head and nose of a lemming are shaped for effective tunneling under snow so that the animal can burrow down to keep warm. The chameleon's body is streamlined to enable it to slip easily through cracks and crevices. The bumpy shapes on a toad's body blend in with the rocks and pebbles on the floor of the forest to better afford the toad protection from enemies.

In summary, animals have varied body features to protect them from weather or to assist them in evading predators. The degree to which animals adapt to their ecosystems is quite amazing!

Two-Part Lesson: Writing a Multiple-Paragraph Composition

Part 2: Writing the composition

EXPLANATION: This part of the lesson picks up from the planning stage and models for students how to use their completed camera graphic organizers to draft their composition. Students should not be expected to use an organizer like this each time they write an informational piece. However, using them initially and then working with them sporadically can help young writers develop good habits.

Skill Focus

Writing informational pieces with multiple paragraphs

Materials & Resources

☆ Students' completed camera graphic organizers, from Part 1 of this lesson

☆ Research notes you have prepared for your topic

Quick Hints

Use this hands-on technique to demonstrate the relationships among ideas in the camera graphic organizer. Empty a jar filled with small rocks and sand into a strainer/colander over a newspaper. Shake the strainer. The small pieces of sand will fall through the holes, but the rocks will remain in the strainer. Point out that the rocks are the key ideas and the sand grains are the details that develop the main ideas.

STEPS

1. Review with students how the camera graphic organizer has helped them plan their informational compositions: The first camera is the big idea; the film frames are the supporting details, examples, and illustrations; and the final camera brings closure by returning to the big idea. Next, read through the five ideas on your own camera graphic from Part 1 of this lesson. Tell students that in this part of the lesson you will turn the information from the organizer into a draft of a composition and then challenge them to do the same with their own organizers.

2. Using a transparency, model your writing process. Start by writing the five sentences from your camera planner, in sequence. Leave several lines of space between each sentence. Point out to your students that these are the lead-in sentences for your five paragraphs.

3. Next, display and refer to notes that you have taken about your own topic. Based on your research notes (which can be quite simple for this lesson) and the framework you have set up (see previous step), model for students how you draft the five paragraphs. When it is complete, read it aloud, calling attention to the logical flow of ideas that your camera graphic has helped you establish. A sample piece, based on the organizer in Part 1, is shown on page 33.

5. Finally, invite students to turn their own camera graphic organizers into good informational pieces, following the same procedure you demonstrated.

Making Writing Cleaner and Clearer (Conventions)

You'll notice that this section on teaching conventions is the longest one in this book. We want to be clear right away that its length is not meant to imply that its content is any more significant than that of other sections. Our firm belief is that while conventions definitely play an important role in good writing, there are other elements of writing that are equally if not more crucial to effective written communication. The length of this chapter is largely due to the level of discreteness contained in most states' standards documents. It is also a response to the fact that the question we most often hear from teachers is, "I have to teach grammar, mechanics, and usage—can I do so in a mini-lesson format?" The answer revealed in this chapter is, "Yes, and you can do it in the context of one of your regular writing model lessons. You can even integrate it with your content studies!"

The research of Hillocks and Smith (2003) has established that isolated grammar instruction, or what these researchers call "traditional school grammar," does not result in a higher degree of correctness, nor does it raise the overall quality of student writing. In fact, writing quality actually *decreases* when teachers place a heavy emphasis on grammar, mechanics, and usage.

On the positive side, research has shown that natural process writing instruction is superior to more traditional grammar instruction in that it improves both the quality and the correctness of students' writing (Hillocks, 1986). With this in mind, and with a firm belief that getting students to use appropriately what we've taught—to transfer learning to other authentic situations—is the ultimate goal of instruction, we look to the Writing Workshop as a mainstay of instruction.

There are several ingredients in a Writing Workshop that facilitate excellent instruction. Perhaps the most important, indeed the one we consider the "magic ingredient," is *authentic context*. As we model writing daily for students, we show them not only *how* to apply the conventions but also *why* we do what we do. Beyond the "how" and "why," we also clearly illustrate for them the power of the application of conventions to our real writing.

We know that underlining pages of subjects and verbs (one line for subjects, two lines for verbs) isn't likely to help students make a connection between that activity and real-world writing. So instead, as we write ourselves, we point out how sentences that express complete thoughts have subjects and verbs. We show students in our own written models that certain verbs are appropriate to use with certain subjects, that certain suffixes on verbs reflect time, and that some verbs are stronger and more expressive than others. In our teaching, we have seen time and again that once students have visible proof that writing becomes clearer, more appropriate for their audience, and far more expressive and powerful, they'll remember to apply what they've learned. The truth is they really do want to produce quality writing, they just need the right kind of guidance along the way.

To lay the groundwork for your instruction, you need to decide on what you consider to be the basic conventions that your students should adhere to daily—even in their draft writing. First, you need to communicate clearly to students that the rough draft is just that—rough! If you overemphasize correctness, your students will quickly get the idea that they can't consider themselves writers until they know all the things that make writing correct. Although it certainly plays a part in communicating effectively, correctness isn't what writing is all about.

That being said, you need to let them know that there are both acceptable and unacceptable degrees of roughness. For a period of time recently, educators referred to the rough draft as the "sloppy copy." Then we realized that this term was encouraging sloppiness! Sloppy isn't what we want. We want a draft that is legible, fairly well organized, and (after we apply certain criteria) relatively free of basic grammar and usage errors.

Display your own established criteria on a chart in your classroom as a constant resource for you and your students. As you model daily, you can refer to this chart or banner, which we call the Quick Check list, as you clean up your rough draft. The students can help you with this. We all know that they're much more critical of our work than they are of their own, so this may be an easy task for them! In any case, it will give them good practice daily.

What are the parameters within which you can establish the basic criteria for your class? Here are some tips for you to consider as you make this decision:

1. Remember that these basics are just that—basics. They aren't necessarily the elements that define quality of writing. These are the elements that make the draft easy for the writer to read back and easy for the reader (you or a peer) to navigate. Higher-quality revisions and more thorough editing will come later in the writing process.

2. Choose only those basic elements that you're willing to encourage daily in your own model writing. You'll want the Quick Check list to be truly quick and easy to apply on a daily basis. In the long run, these are the criteria you want your students to internalize and apply automatically every time they write, even beyond your classroom. If your list is endless, it won't become automatic, and it will likely become an arduous daily task for you as well.

3. Pick your battles—a.k.a. your criteria—wisely! If you put an item on your Quick Check list, you'll have to be willing to hold students accountable to it daily—not just in the Writing Workshop but in all the draft writing that they complete. To avoid a situation in which you wind up having to remind students of a rule needlessly or endlessly, choose only those criteria that are truly essential and doable.

Now, stop and think what you believe are the conventions most essential to students' daily writing. What are your minimum requirements? List them on paper. We would suggest that you limit your list to between eight and ten items. Each item should be so basic that it deserves its very own explicit instruction and mini-lesson. Depending on your particular class and class situation, certain items will be review items for your students (and thus included early in the year) and others will be more sophisticated concepts that can wait a bit. We've incorporated one possible set of criteria for a Quick Check list into a sample chart, shown on page 37.

These are merely suggestions. Every teaching situation is unique, and you're the one who needs to make the decision about what goes on your list.

As you teach a mini-lesson and demonstrate the new point several times, add that concept to your list so that it will be visible in the classroom. One idea is to include each new criterion on a sheet of flip chart paper, one item at a time. Alternately, you might use a pocket chart and add the items on sentence strips. Or you might want to be more creative in the display of your criteria. Just be sure that the list is visible and that it's used daily by you and your students.

After an item is displayed, it becomes an automatic criterion to be applied. Help students understand that each day the class will spend a brief period of time looking at the list to clean up the writing papers before putting them away for that day.

We want to conclude by repeating that yes, we value teaching correct grammar, mechanics, and usage. But it's the unique setting of the Writing Workshop that the enables the instruction of these elements to occur in the context of real writing. Only when students witness how correct grammar, mechanics, and usage can make their writing clearer and more expressive will they have those "aha!" moments that will allow the transfer of what they've learned to their own writing.

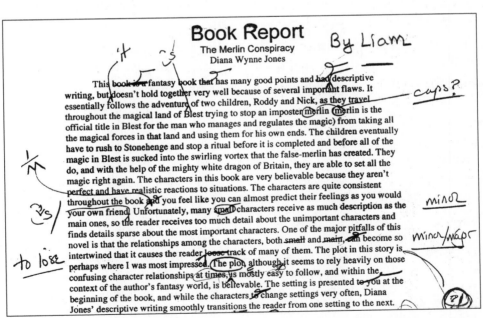

This middle-school student's book report has already been revised for ideas and content. Here the focus is on editing for basic conventions and usage.

Using plurals correctly

EXPLANATION: Most nouns are regular and are made plural by adding s. However, many English words form plurals in unusual ways. This lesson focuses on some of the most common rules for forming irregular plurals. As part of this lesson it will be helpful to provide a chart of the most common rules for forming plurals. In addition, you should have a dictionary available so that students can confirm proper spellings in certain situations.

Skill Focus

Using regular and irregular plurals correctly

Materials & Resources

☆ English handbook for review of rules

☆ Chart of common rules (see Step 1; in addition, check your own local and state standards for specific plural rules)

Quick Hints

Give each student a newspaper article and a highlighter. Challenge students to search for and highlight plural words and to note the appropriate plural rule.

STEPS

1. Using a transparency, chart paper, or the chalkboard, write the following rules for plural usage. Review each rule with the class, eliciting additional examples from volunteers.

Common Plural Rules
1. Most nouns are regular—add *s* to form the plural. Ex: *chairs, plates, desks.*
2. Nouns ending in *ch, sh, s, x,* and *z*—add *es.* Ex: *lunches, ashes, foxes.*
3. Nouns ending in *y* preceded by a consonant—change *y* to *i* and add *es.* Ex: *flies, cries, fries.*
4. Nouns ending in *y* preceded by a vowel—add an *s.* Ex: *days, donkeys, guys.*
5. Some nouns form their plurals by a change in spelling. Ex: *tooth/teeth, foot/feet, mouse/mice.*
6. Some nouns have the same form for both singular and plural. Ex: *deer, sheep, fish, scissors.*
7. Nouns ending in *o* preceded by a consonant vary. With some, add *s,* with others, add *es.* Check the dictionary for correct spellings. Ex: *potato/potatoes, hero/heroes, piano/pianos, solo/solos.*

2. Model writing a paragraph that includes plurals that represent various plural rules. As you write, underline each plural word and discuss the rule that applies. A sample paragraph, with plural words underlined for your convenience, is below.

> James had a report due in science. He decided to write about his pet finches. The public library was full of books, magazines, and brochures that included information about these birds. His teacher taught him to always check the indexes, keys, and other text features to locate information. James zeroed in on the topics of foods, feathers, and habitats. He made copies of the information and used his scissors and glue to cut and paste some neat photos into his report. James was very proud of his work.

3. Invite students to write an original paragraph. Instruct them to include as many plural words as possible. Have them underline the plural words and write them on index cards. Next to each plural word that they record, they should write the number of the rule that applies.

Exploring verb tenses

Skill Focus

Maintaining consistency of verb tense across paragraphs

Materials & Resources

☆ Two text samples: one narrative and one informational (used in this lesson: page 132 of *The Tale of Despereaux* by Kate DiCamillo and page C14 of *Harcourt Science, Grade 5: How Earthquakes Are Measured*) **Note:** The narrative text sample should show consistency in verb tense. Material should be related to your areas of content study, if possible—for example, a literature selection your class is reading and a science textbook you're studying.

Quick Hints

Give students a piece of "dry" informational text (from an old textbook, perhaps) and challenge them to replace the verb constructions with more precise verbs that retain the sense of the piece but that make it more engaging.

STEPS

1. Display the two prepared transparencies of sample text. Ask students to help you highlight verbs that they notice in the two pieces. (It's not really necessary to highlight every verb for this lesson.)

2. Once you've highlighted many of the verbs from the excerpts of text, make a T-chart as shown to the right and list the verbs from each.

Narrative Text	Informational Text
saw	saw
shone	was pulled
stood	traveled
shaded	travels
dressed	is
glittered	has
glowed	marks
captured	use
called	are
watched	releases

3. Follow up by holding a class discussion comparing sentence structure, particularly verb use, in the two different genres. Help focus the discussion by asking questions such as those listed below. If students need further guidance, provide the background information shown in parentheses.

   ☆ What general observations do you have about the types of verbs and verb tenses on the narrative side of the chart? (Writers generally try to keep verb tenses consistent in narrative text because time is an important element within this kind of writing.)

   ☆ What observations do you have about the types of verbs and verb tenses on the informational side of the chart? (If events are referred to in informational text, there is a mixture of verb tenses.)

   ☆ What generalizations can you make to compare the narrative verbs and the verbs from informational text? (Narrative text usually has specific, expressive, or dynamic verbs; informational text has more *to be* verb forms and linking verbs.)

   ☆ Why do you think people sometimes refer to informational text (other than sequenced historical material) as having "timeless verb construction"? (Time is often not an important element in expository writing because most information that is true today— mathematical formulas, geographical locations, nutritional facts, and so on—was also true yesterday and will be true tomorrow.)

   ☆ Does the lack of powerful, expressive verbs in informational text affect how engaging and interesting it is for the reader?

4. Conclude your discussion by summarizing the class's generalizations and comparisons. Remind students that, with the exception of certain special circumstances (such as when events in the past are described in flashbacks), it is important to retain the same verb tense throughout a piece of writing.

Subject-verb agreement

EXPLANATION: Many students feel that writing English correctly is unnatural and complicated, but focused instruction and thoughtful practice can dispel this sentiment. Using English well is a skill and, like most other skills, it can be improved with study and practice. In this lesson, students learn about subject-verb agreement in sentences with a variety of plural subjects.

Skill Focus

Using verbs that agree with plural subjects, including those with compound subjects and with intervening phrases and clauses

Materials & Resources

☆ Prepared transparency of material from especially well-written text (recommended for this lesson: *Appalachia: The Voices of Sleeping Birds* by Cynthia Rylant and *Arthur: The Seeing Stone* by Kevin Crossley-Holland)

Quick Hints

On sentence strips or chart paper write sentences with plural subjects/verbs and intervening clauses or phrases. Use differently colored markers to distinguish the plural subjects/verbs from the intervening clauses or phrases.

Preliminary Considerations: *We recommend using either or both Cynthia Rylant's* Appalachia: The Voices of Sleeping Birds *and* Arthur: The Seeing Stone *by Kevin Crossley-Holland for this lesson because they are both delightfully well-written books, filled with clever examples of writing conventions and craft. You might first read aloud the Rylant book or a few chapters of the Crossley-Holland book for students to enjoy and then reintroduce them in your Writing Workshop for students to analyze. The analysis could provide a whole series of lessons, of which this is only one.*

STEPS

1. Review with students the basic rule of subject-verb agreement: A verb must agree in number with its subject. Thus, all singular subjects take a singular verb; all plural subjects a plural verb. This lesson focuses on sentences with plural subjects and verbs. These plural subjects can come in a variety of forms: as simple plural nouns; as compound subjects (subjects comprising two or more nouns joined by *and*); or as plural pronouns such as *those* and *they*. Explain, too, that students need to watch out for phrases that may come between the subject and the verb. The verb agrees with the subject, not with a noun or a pronoun in the phrase.

2. Tell students that to help them better understand and remember these rules, you want them to examine passages of text from a particularly well-crafted book. Display your prepared transparency of material from Rylant's and Crossley-Holland's books. A sample follows.

Subject-verb agreement with plural subjects
(examples all from *Arthur: The Seeing Stone*)
   p. 42: Two little <u>rooms</u> <u>lead</u> out of the gallery. <u>They</u> <u>are</u> like nests . . .
   p. 46: <u>Merlin and Oliver</u> often <u>argue</u> . . .
   p. 54: In my writing room, <u>snails and beetles and spiders and lice</u> <u>live</u> in most of the little gaps and cracks between the blocks . . .
   p. 129: For a moment, the <u>two men say</u> nothing. <u>They</u> just <u>stand</u> there, on either side of the threshold.

Subject and verb agreement with interrupting phrases and clauses
(examples all from *Appalachia: The Voices of Sleeping Birds*)
   p. 5: <u>Those</u> who do go off, who find some way to become doctors or teachers, nearly always <u>come</u> back to the part of Appalachia where they grew up.
   p. 7: <u>Those</u> who don't live in Appalachia and don't understand it sometimes <u>make</u> the mistake of calling these people "hillbillies."
   p. 11: The <u>kitchens</u> of these houses where Mamie or Boyd or Oley live almost always <u>smell</u> like fried bacon or chicken. . .

3. To conclude this lesson, you might go back to a piece you've written recently and model how you check to be sure that your subjects and subjects and verbs are in agreement. Remind students, as well, to watch for occurrences in their own writing.

A case for pronouns

Skill Focus

Using objective, subjective, and possessive pronouns appropriately

Materials & Resources

☆ Transparency of the composition in this lesson (see Step 1)

☆ Chart of pronoun case rules

☆ Colored transparency pens

Quick Hints

You might want to follow up the true story related in this composition by sharing the Caldecott Award–winning picture book *The Man Who Walked Between the Towers,* by Mordicai Gerstein.

STEPS

1. Explain that pronouns are categorized by what's called "case." The three cases are subjective (pronoun is the subject of the sentence); objective (pronoun is the object); and possessive (pronoun shows ownership). Which pronoun is correct in a sentence depends on how the pronoun is used in that sentence. Using a transparency, chart paper, or the chalkboard, write the following rules for pronoun case:

Pronoun Case	It's used when the pronoun is a	Examples
Subjective (or Nominative)	Subject of a sentence/clause	I, you, he, she, it, they, we
Objective	Direct object, indirect object, object of the preposition	me, you, him, her, it, them, us
Possessive	Word showing possession	my, mine, your, yours, his, her, hers, their, theirs, its, our, ours

2. Next, tell students that the class will examine a draft of a composition that employs many pronouns. Let them know that the writer seems to have had a little confusion in pronoun use. The students' job is to listen to this piece for sense and at the same time to pay close attention to the pronouns. Tell students that afterward they will employ some editing techniques to correct the pronouns. Display your prepared transparency of the following composition and read it aloud. (For your convenience, the relevant pronouns have been highlighted in this sample; your initial presentation of the piece should not include any such markings.)

A Long Walk

Once upon a time, there were two tall towers in New York City, each a quarter of a mile high. A young street performer named Philippe Petit dreamed of walking between the two buildings. <u>He</u> had already walked and danced in several dangerous places such as between the steeples of Notre Dame Cathedral in Paris, where <u>he</u> was arrested.

So, he said to a friend, "<u>I</u> know the police will arrest <u>me</u> if <u>I</u> dare to walk between the Twin Towers. If <u>you</u> help <u>me</u>, <u>you</u> and ~~me~~ could pretend to be construction workers, carrying <u>our</u> supplies to the tops of the buildings. Would <u>you</u> help <u>me</u>, please?" <u>He</u> was so persistent that <u>his</u> friend finally agreed to help.

Late on the night of August 6, 1974, ~~him~~ and <u>his</u> friend, dressed in construction outfits, carried over 400 pounds of cable and other equipment to the tops of both towers. <u>They</u> used a bow and arrow to send rope from one building to the other. ~~Them~~ worked for hours to string the cable across the huge expanse of space.

Finally, as the sun rose the next morning, Philippe was ready to fulfill <u>his</u> dream. As Philippe picked up <u>his</u> balancing pole, his friend called out, "When <u>you</u> walk through the clouds, experience the freedom for <u>you</u> and I̶, too, <u>my</u> friend."

And, Philippe did feel free for the hour and a half that <u>he</u> walked, danced, and even lay down to rest on the wire. The police screamed, and <u>they</u> threatened from both buildings. When Philippe was satisfied, <u>he</u> walked to the police and held out <u>his</u> wrists for the cuffs. But, when <u>he</u> was on the wire in the sky, <u>he</u> had been so completely free.

3. Go back through the composition and, with students' help, underline the pronouns from the chart. Determine how each of the pronouns is being used in the sentence. Then have volunteers consult the chart to be sure that the correct pronoun has been used. Cross out the incorrect pronouns and replace them. (Note: The trickiest error for students to detect and correct will probably be "for you and I." Tell students that when a compound pronoun is used, they should test it by trying to say the sentence with only one subject or object. For example, "When you walk through the clouds, experience the freedom <u>for you and I</u>, too, my friend" would be repeated as "When you walk through the clouds, experience the freedom <u>for I</u>, too, my friend." Without a compound object to distract them, students will be able to hear that *I* is incorrect here.)

Pronoun-antecedent agreement

EXPLANATION: At upper grades, students use pronouns often—and usually correctly—in their spoken and written language. They'll need a few lessons, however, on certain aspects of pronoun use. Here they learn that a pronoun must agree with its antecedent, the noun to which the pronoun refers.

Skill Focus

Making pronouns (including indefinite pronouns) agree with antecedents

Materials & Resources

☆ Chart of common rules (see Step 1; in addition, check your own local and state standards for specific pronoun-antecedent agreement rules)

☆ *The 6th Grade Nickname Game* by Gordon Korman (as resource for sample text)

Quick Hints

Extend the lesson by dividing the class into four groups. Give each group a passage or chapter selection and set a timer to see which group can skim and scan to find the most examples of pronoun-antecedent agreement.

STEPS

1. Review with students that pronouns stand in for nouns to which they refer. Those nouns are called antecedents because they precede (*ante-* and *pre-* both mean "before"), or come before, the pronouns. Pronouns and their antecedents must agree in number. Using a transparency, chart paper, or the chalkboard, write the following rules for pronoun and antecedents:

Rules for Pronoun-Antecedent Agreement
If the antecedent is singular, the pronoun must be singular. **Ex:** <u>Henry</u> lost <u>his</u> coat.
These indefinite pronouns are always singular: *each, either, neither, everyone, everybody, anyone, anybody, someone, somebody, nobody, no one,* and *one.* When an antecedent is modified by *each, every, either,* or *neither,* a singular pronoun must be used to agree with it. **Ex:** <u>Each</u> girl will make <u>her</u> own bracelet.
If the antecedent is plural, the pronoun must be plural. **Ex:** The <u>boys</u> left <u>their</u> bats in the gym.
In a sentence with *neither/nor* or *either/or,* the pronoun must agree with the noun nearest to it. **Ex:** Neither the <u>radios</u> nor the <u>television</u> had <u>its</u> sound turned on.

2. Using a transparency, chart paper, or the chalkboard, model writing a paragraph that includes examples of pronoun-antecedent agreement. Underline each pronoun and its antecedent. A sample paragraph follows.

    I read a good <u>book</u> by Gordon Korman during SSR. <u>It</u> is fast-paced with lots of laughs. <u>It</u> is called *The 6th Grade Nickname Game,* and <u>it</u> is loaded with humor and empathy. <u>Jeff and Wiley</u> are determined to give everyone in <u>their</u> class a nickname. Even <u>each teacher</u> will have <u>his</u> or <u>her</u> own label. Neither the <u>principal</u> nor the English <u>teachers</u> can put a halt to <u>their</u> nickname dubbing. Not <u>everyone</u> is pleased with <u>his</u> or <u>her</u> nickname, and this leads to an interesting twist in the end.

3. Discuss each example and ask the students to identify the rule.

4. Invite students to write an original paragraph. Instruct them to include at least three sentences with pronouns and antecedents.

Comparative and superlative forms of adjectives

EXPLANATION: Very often students will need to understand the comparative and superlative forms of adjectives when doing their own writing. This lesson allows students to have fun as they explore the technical aspects of adjectives and their forms.

Skill Focus

Using comparative and superlative forms of adjectives

Materials & Resources

☆ Pictures of three familiar superheroes (suggested for this lesson: Superman, the Incredible Hulk, and Spider-man; copies of pictures of just about any superhero can be obtained on the Internet and printed in color onto your transparency)

Quick Hints

This activity is quite versatile. Instead of superheroes, you might use pictures from sources that connect to your content areas or famous art masterpieces such as *Starry Night* by Van Gogh or *Dance Class at the Opera* by Degas.

STEPS

1. Review with your students the purpose of an adjective. An adjective is most frequently used to describe a noun or a pronoun.

2. Display the picture of one superhero you've chosen—for example, Superman. Tell your students that you're going to set a timer for three minutes and you want them (independently or with peers) to jot down every adjective they can to describe this picture.

3. While students are working, draw the following chart on the board:

3 FORMS OF ADJECTIVES		
Positive (doesn't compare)	Comparative (compares 2 things; ends with -*er*)	Superlative (compares 3 or more things; ends with -*est*)

4. Have students share with the class the adjectives they've brainstormed. Write all appropriate ones—such as *strong, smart, young, fast,* and *muscular*—in the column labeled "Positive."

5. Call students' attention to the three categories on the chart and explain that there are three forms of adjectives:
   ☆ Positive adjectives, such as the ones they've listed, don't provide comparisons but merely describe.
   ☆ Comparative adjectives have an -*er* suffix and compare two things.
   ☆ Superlative adjectives have an -*est* suffix and compare three or more things.

6. Now display the pictures of the other two superheroes you've selected. Follow the same procedure described in Steps 2 and 4, this time challenging students to use the adjectives they listed for the first hero and to come up with comparisons for the second and the third. The first row of the completed chart might look like that below. **Note:** Some adjectives that students brainstorm will undoubtedly form their comparatives by using *more* rather than adding -*er* and their superlatives by using *most* rather than -*est*. Be prepared to discuss these variant constructions with students.

3 FORMS OF ADJECTIVES		
Positive (doesn't compare)	Comparative (compares 2 things; ends with -*er*)	Superlative (compares 3 or more things; ends with -*est*)
Superman is strong.	Superman is stronger than the Hulk.	Superman is the strongest of the three superheroes.

Comparing with adverbs

EXPLANATION: In this lesson students learn another way to form comparisons—by using adverbs. Adverbs are more difficult than adjectives for most students to grasp. Adjectives modify concrete words, nouns, and pronouns; adverbs modify other adverbs, adjectives, and verbs. And when using adverbs to compare, students must learn in addition that there are three constructions possible.

Skill Focus

Using adverb comparisons correctly

Materials & Resources

☆ Old newspapers and magazines

Quick Hints

Invite students to work in small groups to design advertisements for a new invention or to describe a book recommended for reading. Challenge them to include as many adverb comparatives as possible.

STEPS

1. Tell students that, in addition to adjectives, adverbs can form comparisons. Remind students that adverbs modify only verbs, adjectives, and other adverbs. With this rule in mind, explain to students that adverbs form comparisons in three distinct ways:

   a. Some short adverbs add *-er* or *-est*.

   b. Most adverbs (including those that end in *-ly*) form the comparative with the word *more* and the superlative with the word *most*.

   c. Some adverbs change completely to form the comparative and superlative.

2. Using a transparency or the chalkboard, model writing a short advertisement describing an object, such as a new vacuum cleaner. Incorporate as many different kinds of comparative adverbs as possible in your ad. Underline these adverbs as you write the paragraph. A sample follows.

   > We can promise that the Whirlwind Vacuum Cleaner, Model 200, will make you feel <u>happier</u> than you've felt using any other vacuum cleaner! This powerful machine retracts dirt from carpets <u>more quickly</u> than others do. When compared to Model 100 and Model 150, this vacuum cleans <u>fastest</u> and <u>most thoroughly</u>. Even your <u>worst</u> worn carpets will look <u>better</u>, and your pocketbook will thank you.

3. With the class, analyze each adverb example. Because adverbs can be tricky to identify as well as difficult to differentiate from adjectives, reinforce for students that it is the word's function in the sentence, and not necessarily the word itself, that makes it an adverb. For example, the word *fastest* is an adverb because it modifies *cleans*. If the sentence had read, "fastest vacuum cleaner," the same word would be an adjective.

4. Identify the kind of adverb construction each underlined word represents (refer to list in Step 1).

happier: **a**	most thoroughly: **b**
more quickly: **b**	worst: **c**
fastest: **a**	better: **c**

5. Invite students to search for newspaper and magazine advertisements that make comparisons with adverbs. Have them identify which of the three adverb constructions is used.

Understanding conjunctions

EXPLANATION: While the primary goal of this lesson is instruction on the use of the three kinds of conjunctions, it also includes two "extras." Students are exposed to valuable word study (about the terms for the different kinds of conjunctions), and they learn a fascinating spelling tidbit as well!

Skill Focus

Using conjunctions to connect ideas

Materials & Resources

☆ Chart of relevant prefixes and roots

☆ List of conjunctions (Appendix, page 115)

Quick Hints

As occasional practice, give students a few sentences and challenge them to combine the information in the sentences in as many ways as possible using conjunctions. Suppose you were to give them these two sentences: "Superman is considered by some to be the strongest superhero. Spiderman is a superhero, too." They might write: "Both Superman and Spiderman are superheroes, but Superman is considered to be the stronger one" or "Although Spiderman is a strong superhero, Superman is considered to be stronger" or . . .

STEPS

1. On a transparency or the chalkboard, write the word *conjunction*. Explain that a conjunction is a part of speech like a noun, a verb, or an adjective. It joins words or groups of words in different ways. Add that there are three types of conjunctions: *coordinating, correlative,* and *subordinating.* Write these terms as well.

2. Because all four terms have familiar Latin origins and can be broken fairly easily into prefixes and base words, it might be helpful to explore them using a chart like the one below. Help students guess how the three kinds of conjunctions are alike and different. (All conjunctions connect sentence parts. Coordinating conjunctions connect equal parts; correlative conjunctions connect equal parts with two words that relate to each other; subordinating conjunctions connect one clause to another, less important clause.)

Word or Word Part	Meaning	Example in Paragraph
con-	together; with	
-junction	intersection	
co-	with; equal	
sub-	below	
correlative	naturally related	both/and, neither/nor
coordinating	bringing into a common action	and, or
subordinating	treating as less important	after, when, although

3. Now tell students that you're going to share a brief composition describing a common spelling problem. Underline the conjunctions as you write. The sample paragraph follows.

   <u>When</u> I'm writing, I occasionally come across a word that gives me a problem with its spelling. Typically, I'll sound it out, spell it the best I can, <u>and</u> keep writing. Later, <u>after</u> I look it up in the dictionary, I'm often perplexed to find the word had a silent letter I hadn't suspected. I've always wondered, <u>but</u> I haven't figured out yet, why it's necessary to have so many silent letters in the English language. In fact, there are 26 letters in our alphabet, <u>and</u> 24 of them appear silently in some word! Amazing! <u>Both</u> writers <u>and</u> readers are often surprised by these sneaky little letters. <u>Neither</u> logic <u>nor</u> phonics can help us with some words.

4. With the class, identify each conjunction, analyzing which kind of conjunction it represents. Remind students of the basic job that conjunctions perform: They greatly enhance sentence variety and thus allow our writing to go beyond boring simple sentences. Refer students to a list of conjunctions in the Appendix (page 115).

5. At last, have students guess the two "sneaky little letters" of the alphabet that don't have silent spellings (*j* and *v*).

Elaborating with prepositional phrases

Skill Focus

Using prepositional phrases to elaborate

Materials & Resources

☆ Previously-written student compositions

Quick Hints

Working in small groups, students can share selections from their independent reading. Have them search for and identify prepositional phrases used by these authors. Challenge them to explain to their peers how the phrases help elaborate ideas and smooth out the writing.

STEPS

1. Review with students that a prepositional phrase includes the preposition itself, its object, and all the words that describe the object. Use several examples, such as "behind the last door," "into the rushing river," and "between the two cars," to help students grasp these concepts.

2. On a transparency or the chalkboard, write a simple paragraph with short, choppy sentences. A sample is below.

   Mr. Montgomery is the high school football coach. He thinks the football team is good. The team has experience. His players are talented. There are two excellent quarterbacks. The punter broke the kicking record. He kicked the ball 58 yards. The team averaged 183 yards on offense. The result should be a winning season.

3. Read the paragraph aloud and elicit reactions from the class. Students should realize that the paragraph is very choppy and awkward. Next, rewrite the paragraph, adding prepositional phrases that elaborate and connect the ideas, making the writing smoother. Underline the phrases, compare the two paragraphs, and discuss the differences with students.

   Mr. Montgomery is the high school football coach. In his opinion, his team has a real chance. His players are talented, with two excellent quarterbacks. The punter broke the school kicking record by kicking the ball 58 yards. With an average of 183 yards on offense, the team can expect a winning season.

4. Finally, direct students to select a paragraph or brief composition from their writing folders and to revise it by turning sentences into prepositional phrases or by adding prepositional phrases to the sentences already there. This is a good opportunity to call students' attention to the revision process and to discuss how revising helps improve writing.

Using appositives

EXPLANATION: Students in the intermediate grades are ready for to introduce some technical grammatical elements into their writing. You might want to let your students know that they will likely impress their readers with their level of sophistication by using technical elements in their writing. And naturally, you want your students to understand that using technical elements like appositives will help make their writing clearer to readers.

Skill Focus

Using appositives appropriately; using commas with appositives

Materials & Resources

☆ Colored transparency pens

☆ Photocopies (one for each student) of the comma usage handout (Appendix, page 117)

Quick Hints

To offer students additional practice with appositives, give them a list of familiar names— musicians, school faculty and staff, movie stars, and so on. Challenge them to write sentences that include the person's name along with an identifying appositive.

STEPS

1. Tell students that today's lesson deals with a helpful writing element called an *appositive*. Appositives are expressions that rename or identify preceding nouns or pronouns. Usually we use commas to set off an appositive. There are two exceptions to this rule: (1) Commas are not used if the appositive is restrictive (necessary to the meaning), and (2) commas are optional for one- or two-word appositives. Depending on your students' strengths and needs, you might introduce these exceptions now or wait until the conclusion of the lesson, when you feel they have developed a firmer grasp of the basic tenets.

2. Using a transparency or the chalkboard, write a brief passage that includes several appositives. Ask students to search for the appositives as you write. Then have volunteers come forward to underline these expressions with a colored transparency pen (or colored chalk). A sample paragraph that includes four appositives— and a bit of interesting trivia—follows. (For your convenience, the appositives have been underlined in this sample; your initial presentation of the piece should not include any such markings.)

Stephen King: Rags to Riches*

Stephen King, <u>a writer famous for his chilling novels</u>, spent much of his life growing up in Maine. In fact, Bangor, <u>a small city in the heart of Maine</u>, is the model for many of his thrilling tales. King worked there at a coin-operated laundry for $1.60 an hour. Supposedly, he based the mother in *Carrie*, <u>his first big hit</u>, on a woman he met there. King lived nearby in a rundown house, <u>the only place he could afford</u>. It was there that he received notification of the acceptance of his work by a publisher. He received the news by telegram because he was too poor to have a phone. Obviously, circumstances are a bit different for Mr. King today!

3. Ask students to notice the punctuation used for these explanatory expressions. Call on other volunteers to come forward and circle (with a pen or chalk of a different color) the pairs of commas that enclose each appositive. Point out that the last appositive has only an introductory comma and ends with the period.

4. To conclude the lesson, provide students with a handout of appropriate uses of commas (see Appendix, p. 117). Have them keep the handout in their writing notebook so that they can consult it when they're in doubt about a comma's use. It will be useful right away in the next lesson, as well as in their everyday writing.

* Based on information from an article in *The State Newspaper* (6/29/05).

Using commas after introductory phrases and clauses

EXPLANATION: In this lesson students continue work with correct placement of commas in sentences. Here they learn the rules that govern comma use with introductory phrases and clauses.

Skill Focus

Using commas after clauses and longer introductory phrases

Materials & Resources

☆ Previously-written student compositions

Quick Hints

During individual conferences, ask students to circle commas in a piece of their writing and then to explain why the commas are needed in those instances.

STEPS

1. Tell students that writers sometimes set the stage for their readers with an introductory phrase or clause before stating the main content of a sentence. Explain that when students do this in their writing, they should use a comma to set off the introduction from the main part of the sentence. Further explain that introductory clauses, which have both a subject and a verb, always require a comma. Introductory phrases, which don't have both a subject and a verb, may or may not require a comma. Long ones usually do, and short ones usually don't.

2. Using a transparency or the chalkboard, display examples of sentences with clauses or introductory phrases and the appropriate comma usage. Underline the clauses and phrases as you write, and engage the class in a discussion about why the commas are used in these sentences.

Sentences with introductory clause:

<u>When you return the call</u>, be sure to tell Ray that practice is at 6 p.m.

<u>As we walk into the museum</u>, try to remain quiet.

<u>Now that the coach has posted the rules</u>, we know what to do.

Sentences with introductory phrases:

<u>On his way through the long hallway on the first floor</u>, Mr. Ford called to remind me to lock the door.

<u>On the highest shelf in the high school's main library</u>, you will find the latest book by Mem Fox.

<u>In the dirty overflowing lake water</u>, there appears to be much debris.

In 1984 I got my hair cut. [Note: For this short introductory phrase, no comma is used.]

3. Direct students to do a quick write for approximately five minutes. Have them add introductory phrases or clauses to sentences where appropriate. Instruct students to circle the comma after each phrase or clause.

4. Finally, instruct students to browse through compositions from their writing folders and to identify introductory phrases and clauses used in those pieces. Have them check to see if the comma was used correctly and, if it wasn't, to make the necessary corrections.

Using dialogue and quotation marks for conversation

EXPLANATION: Dialogue is one of the best devices writers can employ to bring life and voice to their writing. Most students in the intermediate grades have experimented with writing dialogue, but most still need a great deal of practice to use it effectively. This lesson gives them a model and a fun practice exercise.

Skill Focus

Using quotation marks in conversation

Materials & Resources

☆ Transparency of a comic strip from a newspaper (a strip with several frames of dialogue is best); comic strip should be reproduced at the top of the transparency ahead of time, leaving blank space for writing below

☆ Transparency markers

☆ Additional comic strips from newspaper (one strip per partner group), either reproduced on transparencies or simply clipped out

Quick Hints

Keep a folder full of cartoons, especially the longer ones from Sunday's paper, in your writing center. Encourage students to change the comic strips into narrative form. This will help them develop confidence in the use of dialogue.

STEPS

1. Using the transparency you've prepared, display your chosen comic strip.

2. On the space beneath the strip, write out the cartoon in narrative format. Convert the cartoon's conversation bubbles into several possible narrative dialogue formats, each showing the correct use of quotation marks. Below are a few possible formats.

Interrupted dialogue:

"When I'm your age, Mr. Wilson," shouted Denise, "I want to take naps just like you!"

Quotation occurring before speaker's name:

"When I'm your age, Mr. Wilson, I want to take naps just like you!" shouted Denise.

Quotation occurring after speaker's name:

Denise shouted, "When I'm your age, Mr. Wilson, I want to take naps just like you!"

3. Call students' attention to the use and correct placement of the commas and punctuation marks in each example. Discuss, too, that in writing we usually indent each time the speaker changes. Explain that this is another signal to help readers know who's speaking.

4. Now give each partner group of students a comic strip. (You might give the same strip to all students or a different one to each group.) Allow several minutes for students to change the strip's dialogue bubbles into narratives using quotations, following the models you have provided.

5. Invite groups to share their work with the rest of the class. If their copies are on transparencies, you can use the overhead projector to display each group's strip. Otherwise, groups might pass their example around the room for classmates to examine.

Using apostrophes correctly

EXPLANATION:
Intermediate-level students are familiar with the use of possessive words to show ownership, but they still can benefit from review of the rules governing apostrophe placement. In this lesson they have the opportunity to practice identifying and using those rules—first in a model paragraph and then in a piece of original writing.

Skill Focus

Using apostrophes with singular and plural possessives

Materials & Resources

☆ Transparency or chart of the rules for forming possessives (see Step 1)

Quick Hints

Look back over student writing from previous years and select pieces that use possessives. Make a transparency of the writing (be sure to omit the writer's name) to model how to locate and underline the possessives. Ask students to assist in editing for correct possessive usage. Allow students to work in pairs to apply their knowledge to other pieces of writing.

STEPS

1. Remind students that a possessive noun shows who or what owns something. Display your transparency or chart of the following rules for using apostrophes to form possessives and review them with your students:

   I. To form the possessive of a singular noun, add an apostrophe (') and an *s*. Ex: *bike—bike's tires*

   II. To form the possessive of a plural noun, there are two rules to remember:

      a. If the plural noun ends in an *s*, simply add the apostrophe to the end of the word. Ex: *boys—boys' gym shorts*

      b. If the plural noun does not end in *s*, then add an apostrophe and an *s*. Ex: *men—men's watches*

2. Using a transparency, chart paper, or the chalkboard, display a paragraph that incorporates possessives. As you write, underline each possessive word. A sample follows. (You might want to point out that in this example, although the first underlined word ends in *s*, it is a singular noun; therefore, it follows the regular rule for adding an apostrophe and an *s*.)

   ### Our Class's Celebration

   Our <u>class's</u> celebration at the end of the year was awesome! <u>Tyler's</u> book review was the best ever. The <u>girls'</u> geography project took top honors! The teachers were delighted to hear the <u>children's</u> quartet sing songs from the Roaring Twenties. We will have to work hard to make next <u>year's</u> celebration even better.

3. Identify each possessive used and the possessive rule to follow.
   - class's—Rule 1
   - Tyler's—Rule 1
   - girls'—Rule 2a
   - children's—Rule 2b
   - year's—Rule 1

4. Ask students to write an original paragraph that incorporates at least one example of each of the three possessive rules taught in this lesson. Have them title it with a possessive phrase, such as "My Friend's Dog" or "The Boys' Party."

Listing with colons

STEPS

1. Tell students that this lesson focuses on the colon. Explain (or review) that the colon is a punctuation mark composed of two dots, one over the other. Among the many ways a colon is used is to precede a list of items. In this case, the colon serves as a kind of transition between the introduction to the list and the list itself. (For other uses of the colon, refer students to the Appendix, page 115.)

2. Tell students that you're going to make a chart of things that interest you. Each chart entry in the left-hand column is an introductory statement that you will fill in with a list of relevant items. Using your transparency, first present the chart without colons (see end of this lesson for a sample chart). Explain that there's a punctuation mark that's needed in each of your sentences. Next, model for students how you add colons in the appropriate place after each introductory statement.

3. Brainstorm some of your answers and add them after the colons. Be sure students realize that the far left column leads into the middle column and, for each row, forms a distinct sentence. For that reason, each entry in the middle column should end with a period. (In the sample chart, the first example row has been filled in. It's not necessary for you to fill out the whole chart in this lesson.) Leave the third column blank at this point.

4. Distribute a chart to each student. Instruct students to add colons to the end of each sentence introduction in the first column. Remind them of why this is necessary.

5. Set a timer and give students about ten minutes to fill out the second column of their charts.

6. Direct students' attention back to your transparency and model filling in the third column. Reset the timer for ten minutes and instruct students to move around the room to elicit feedback for the third column from as many students as possible. If another student has an identical interest/item listed on his or her own chart, that student should write in his or her first name in the third column.

EXPLANATION:
This is a good lesson to use fairly early in the school year. Not only does it teach students about one of the uses of the colon but it also enables them to get to know each other a little better.

Skill Focus

Using colons to introduce a list; Using commas appropriately

Materials & Resources

☆ Transparency of a model chart

☆ Photocopied charts (one for each student; use the one below as a template, omitting the colons)

☆ Colon use chart (see Appendix, page 115)

Quick Hints

Have students file their completed chart in their writing folder for reference when they need a topic to write about. Point out that by referring to the chart, they'll gain further information: the names of others who might be ideal collaborators in writing or revising/editing a topical piece.

Introductory statements	My list	A list of friends who share my interests
These are things I know a lot about:	skiing, playing the violin, reading, and dogs.	Ms. Brown, Mr. Weinstock, Ms. McManamy
Here are careers I might consider:		
These are songs and musicians I like:		
Here are some TV shows I watch:		
These are books I read and liked:		
These are some things I like to do:		
Here are places I've visited:		
These are places I'd like to visit:		

Using semicolons correctly

STEPS

EXPLANATION:
Intermediate students, already quite familiar with many of the ways commas can be used in sentences, are now ready to learn about another way to combine sentence parts—the semicolon. This lesson gives them instruction and experience with two of the three uses of this punctuation mark.

Skill Focus

Using semicolons to connect main clauses; Using commas appropriately

Materials & Resources

☆ Transparency or display chart with rules for semicolon use

Quick Hints

Provide students with samples of real-life materials (such as travel brochures or summer camp pamphlets) that contain semicolons. Challenge them to search for uses of semicolons. Have students work in pairs to circle the semicolons with a red pen and discuss whether the connection was made with or without a conjunction.

1. Explain to students that today's lesson will focus on the correct use of another punctuation mark—the semicolon. Display for students your transparency or chart showing the three primary uses for semicolons to connect clauses in writing.

   Semicolons
   * connect independent clauses without a conjunction,
   * connect independent clauses with certain conjunctive words, such as *however* and *therefore* (technically known as conjunctive adverbs),
   * connect word groups that contain commas.

2. This lesson will focus on the first two rules—connecting independent clauses without conjunctions and also with certain conjunctions.

3. Using a transparency or the chalkboard, write a paragraph with sentences that illustrate how semicolons are used to connect independent clauses (the first and second rules above). A sample paragraph follows.

   > Robert began to walk toward the car; nothing could make him turn back. He was desperate to escape, although upset to leave his clothes and belongings behind. He had hurried to make plans from the moment he heard about the hurricane; however, it was already 7 p.m. and the eye of the hurricane was supposed to arrive at 7:45. The trees were straining under the force of the wind. The sheets of rain came in waves; water quickly became ankle deep. Departing before nightfall was critical, as his destination was unknown.

4. Call attention to the semicolons as you write, and discuss with the class why the semicolons are needed for these sentences. Discuss, too, why commas are correct—rather than semicolons—for the second and the final sentence (neither sentence contains two independent clauses).

5. Invite students to write a paragraph telling where Robert might be going to escape the hurricane. Ask them to include at least two sentences that use semicolons to combine independent clauses. As a bonus, you might challenge students to include a sentence that follows the third rule for semicolons, which was not dealt with explicitly in this lesson.

Capitalizing appropriately

EXPLANATION: This lesson emphasizes a variety of rules governing capitalization. Students will already be familiar with a number of these rules (such as for the first word in a sentence and for names), but other uses (such as for direct quotes and sentences quoted within sentences) will be less familiar. These further uses can prove valuable as students add new, more sophisticated elements to their own writing.

Skill Focus

Capitalizing words, including quotations and proper nouns, correctly

Materials & Resources

☆ Handout (one for each student) of the rules for capitalization (see Appendix, page 116)

Quick Hints

To keep students on their toes about the fine points of capitalization, occasionally engage them in the following activity. Assign each partner group of students a different, quite specific rule of capitalization—for example, "Use capital letters with musical compositions." Give each pair a newspaper and see how many examples of that rule they can locate and highlight. Then have them share some of their examples with the class.

STEPS

1. Tell students that this lesson focuses on certain applications of a punctuation skill already familiar to them as writers and readers—correct capitalization. Display these rules for the four uses you'll highlight today:

   Capitalize
   - the first word of a sentence,
   - specific names of people (proper nouns),
   - brand names of products (proper nouns),
   - the first word of directly quoted speech.

2. Share with students that you've read a short account of the invention of the Band-Aid. The invention is attributed to Earle Dickson in 1920. Mr. Dickson's wife evidently had so many kitchen accidents that he had to do something about it! You've decided to write a short scene depicting how this event may have taken place—just as historical fiction writers do. An example passage follows.

   "I've cut my hand yet again," wept the young wife as she wrapped her hand in a kitchen towel. "I'm so clumsy!"

   "Don't worry, dear," said the husband, consoling his wife. "You work so long and hard in this kitchen, caring for our family. These cuts are bound to happen."

   "Here I've spoiled another towel," the wife said as she cried even harder. "I stained it with blood from my cut."

   "There must be a better solution," the husband thought out loud, "for caring for little wounds. I have an idea!"

   Thus, the Band-Aid we use today was born—an invention by Earle Dickson in 1920 for his wife. As the saying goes, "Necessity is the mother of invention!"

3. Go back through the piece, highlighting the different ways capitalization is used. Have students discuss examples of each of the four rules above.

4. Remember that the rules of capitalization are almost too numerous to expect students at this grade level to remember, especially in their rough draft writing! Continue to teach and reinforce the rules. As further support, distribute a handout of the complete rules for capitalization, which students can refer to independently, especially in their editing work. (See Appendix, page 116.)

Using a variety of sentence structures and lengths

EXPLANATION: Many successful authors employ a variety of sentence structures and lengths. Simple sentences, which are usually short, can serve to punctuate text and make points dramatically. Compound and complex sentences, which are usually longer, allow writing to flow smoothly. Students can use the models provided in this lesson to revise their own writing.

Skill Focus

Using a variety of sentence structures and lengths

Materials & Resources

☆ Preselected passage from a well-crafted children's book (used in this lesson: *Number the Stars* by Lois Lowry)

Quick Hints

Select a poem such as "Where the Sidewalk Ends" by Shel Silverstein. Ask students to change the simple sentences to compound or complex sentences and the compound or complex sentences to simple ones. Have them read aloud the rewritten poem and discuss how it sounds compared to the original.

STEPS

1. Review with students the three different kinds of sentence structures: *simple* (one main clause), *compound* (two or more independent clauses), and *complex* (main clause and one or more subordinate clauses). Tell students that this lesson will give them experience using these different structures and also varying sentence length. Discuss how encountering a variety of sentence formats makes text more interesting and engaging for readers.

2. Using a transparency or the chalkboard, display an excerpt from a well-respected children's author. Go through the passage with students and help them identify the different sentence structures. A sample passage from Lois Lowry's *Number the Stars* (page 2) follows. (The correct identifications are provided in parentheses for your convenience; your initial presentation of the piece should not include any such markings.)

   > "*Halte!*" the soldier ordered in a stern voice. (*simple*)
   > . . . Annemarie had heard it often enough before, but it had never been directed at her until now. (*compound*)
   > Behind her, Ellen also slowed and stopped. (*simple*) Far back, little Kirsti was plodding along, her face in a pout because the girls hadn't waited for her. (*complex*)
   > Annemarie stared up. (*simple*) . . . She stared at the rifles first. (*simple*) Then, finally, she looked into the face of the soldier who had ordered her to halt. (*complex*)

3. Explain that simple sentences are usually short, while compound and complex sentences can run quite long. Discuss the effect the simple sentences have on the reader. Take, for example, "Annemarie stared up. . . . She stared at the rifles first." These short simple sentences seem to jolt the reader. Next, discuss how the compound and complex sentences act to keep the reader moving along. The text seems to flow with these sentences.

4. Next, write a list of several simple sentences. Model for students how you can combine them to create compound and complex sentences. A sample list and paragraph based on the list follow.

   > Melissa was his next-door neighbor.
   > Her nickname was Missa.
   > James called her Melissa.
   > She was his best friend.
   > He went to visit her often.
   > She baked cookies to share with him.
   > They were soft and gooey.

   > Melissa was his next-door neighbor. (*simple*) Her nickname was Missa, but James called her Melissa. (*compound*) She was his best friend. (*simple*) He visited her often because she baked soft, gooey cookies and always shared them. (*complex*)

4. Have students write their own simple sentences and then combine them into compound and complex ones.

Using a variety of sentence types

EXPLANATION: Although we teach students that they should vary their sentences in their writing, we don't want to give the impression that they should strive to use all the different sentence options in each piece of writing. Instead, we want students to be aware of the different possibilities and to understand how certain sentences lend themselves better to certain purposes. Here we add to students' repertoire by exploring the four types of sentences—declarative, interrogative, exclamatory, and imperative.

Skill Focus

Using a variety of sentence types (imperative, interrogative, exclamatory, declarative)

Materials & Resources

☆ Four transparency pens (different colors)

☆ Optional: a banana, a knife (plastic for safety reasons)

Quick Hints

Organize the class into small groups and assign each one a type of sentence. Challenge them to brainstorm a list of the kinds of writing in which they would most likely encounter that type of sentence. Have the group then write a brief passage within one of those writing formats. Encourage groups to share their findings and their passages.

STEPS

Note: *Be forewarned that students will undoubtedly want to try the experiment described in this lesson. So you might want to be prepared with a banana and a cutting instrument and set some time aside after the lesson. (Remember safety issues!) One possibility is to have students reread the directions as you perform the experiment; another option is for you to do the rereading, while a particularly responsible student tries out the experiment.*

1. Tell students that you're going to share a neat trick with them through your writing today. (With their parents' permission, this might even be something they experiment with at breakfast tomorrow morning!) Using a transparency or the chalkboard, write the following passage (note that the correct identifications are indicated for your convenience; they should not be included in your original presentation):

   Have you ever been faced with the task of dividing food to share with family or friends at the dinner table? (*interrogative*) You try really hard to be fair to everyone and not to make one piece or helping bigger than another. (*declarative*) Well, I'm thinking of one food that causes a real dilemma. (*declarative*) What if you were asked to divide a banana among three people? (*interrogative*) Oh, my! (*interjection*) What would you do? (*interrogative*)

   Just in case you're ever faced with this problem, there's a trick to splitting a banana three equal ways. (*declarative*) First, cut off a small chunk from the stem end of the banana and discard that piece. (*imperative*) Then, peel the banana from the top about halfway down. (*imperative*) Next, put your index finger in the base of the banana where you cut the small slice off. (*imperative*) Push your finger up into the core of the banana. (*imperative*) There you are! (*exclamatory*) Much to everyone's surprise, the banana will split into three equal pieces! (*exclamatory*)

2. Model checking back through your composition. Tell students that you've noticed that you've used four different types of sentences in writing this piece. Define the four sentence types for students as follows:

   Imperative: This sentence makes a command or gives an order. It often starts with an action verb and typically ends with a period or possibly an exclamation point. The subject in an imperative sentence is you, but it is usually not stated directly.

   Declarative: This sentence merely makes a statement and ends with a period. It is the most common type of sentence.

   Interrogative: This sentence asks a question and ends with a question mark.

   Exclamatory: This sentence shows strong emotion and ends with an exclamation point.

3. Before focusing on the sentences, point out that there's one tricky element in this passage. It isn't a real sentence (i.e., it doesn't have a subject, a verb, or express a complete thought). Challenge students to identify it and to name it, if possible. If they need further guidance, explain that it's "Oh, my!" in the first paragraph and that it is called an *interjection*. Interjections are short expressions that appear as sentences but that merely express emotion. "Yikes!" is another common interjection.

4. Now, invite volunteers to come up to the overhead projector, underline, and identify each sentence by type (highlighting each type with a designated color). As students do this, engage the class in a discussion about the sentences and what characteristics make them fit into a certain category.

Avoiding fragments and run-ons

Skill Focus

Avoiding fragments and run-ons

Materials & Resources

☆ Selection of text that incorporates fragments and run-ons

Quick Hints

In your classroom library, make available a few copies of *Canyons* by well-respected children's author Gary Paulsen. Alert students to Paulsen's deliberate use of fragments and run-ons. Have them search for these and discuss with partners what special effect the author achieves by incorporating them. Remind students that these errors are not allowed in conventional writing.

STEPS

1. Tell students that this lesson highlights a common problem: fragments and run-on sentences. Review the following definitions:
   - A *fragment* is a group of words that do not sound complete. The subject or predicate is usually missing. Ex: *Running a race.*
   - A *run-on* sentence occurs when two or more sentences run together as one sentence because punctuation is missing or has been used incorrectly. Ex: *The fish we catch in the lake will be our food, they will be delicious.*

2. Using a transparency or the chalkboard, select or write a paragraph that contains examples of fragments and run-ons. A sample follows.

Monarch Butterflies and Atlantic Green Turtles

The Monarch butterfly and the Atlantic green turtle rely on their instincts to migrate. The butterfly spends the summer in the northeastern United States, the southwest coast of Canada, or Washington and Oregon. These interesting creatures relocate in the winter. To central Mexico, Florida, or the coast of California. On the other hand, the Atlantic green turtle migrates from the coast of Brazil to Ascension Island in the South Atlantic Ocean. The butterfly cannot survive in subfreezing areas, it flies in search of trees, a moderate climate, and plentiful water. Unlike the butterfly. The turtles swim to the island to lay their eggs and then to the Brazilian coast to rich feeding areas. Monarch butterflies and Atlantic green turtles are able to survive because of their varying instincts.

3. Isolate the sentence errors and discuss how to correct them.

   - **Fragment:** To central Mexico, Florida, or the coast of California.

   Solution: Combine the fragment with the sentence preceding it.

   Resulting Sentence: These interesting creatures relocate in winter to central Mexico, Florida, or the coast of California.

   - **Run-On:** The butterfly cannot survive in subfreezing areas, it flies in search of trees, a moderate climate, and plentiful water.

   Solution: Use a conjunctive adverb (*therefore*) and a semicolon to join ideas.

   Resulting Sentence: The butterfly cannot survive in subfreezing areas; therefore, it flies in search of trees, a moderate climate, and plentiful water.

   - **Fragment:** Unlike the butterfly.

   Solution: Combine the fragment with the sentence following it.

   Resulting Sentence: Unlike the butterfly, the turtles swim to the island to lay their eggs and then to the Brazilian coast to rich feeding areas.

4. Have students write about a self-selected topic for approximately ten minutes. Then have them evaluate their writing for sentence fragments and run-ons and make corrections using the models.

Making Writing Better (Revision)

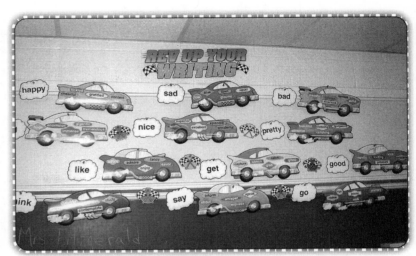

Revision is one of those words that we probably don't take literally enough. *Re-vision* is exactly that—looking at a first draft again in a different way. This is the stage at which a writer looks at a piece of writing and decides that he or she needs to make certain changes to improve its quality and effectiveness.

The youngest writers, oddly enough, are usually quite satisfied with their initial attempts at writing—not only because they're inexperienced but because they feel that they've put enough energy into the draft. For these beginning writers, writing is quite laborious—both mentally and physically. Because their fine motor skills aren't fully developed, they're expending a lot of energy just in making basic letter formations. They see revision as tidying up their writing a bit—which really isn't revision at all.

One of our key jobs as teachers in the Writing Workshop is to dispel the notion that tidiness—correctness—is what it's all about. As we discussed in the previous section, we certainly need to let our students know that correctness counts. Even in their rough draft writing they need to be aware of and apply basic conventions well. And ultimately, for pieces they will polish and take to a higher level of completion—and perhaps even publish—they will need to correct mistakes. Editing (discussed in Section Six) will give them that opportunity.

But in between they need to know that many other elements also count in producing quality writing. Revision is the time to cut and paste, mold and rework for sense and flow, reword and rewrite for liveliness and language use. It's the time to see the potential in one's words, to take that diamond in the rough and really shape it into something valuable. Editing for correctness makes our work cleaner and easier to read, but only real revising gives it quality and makes it a pleasure to read.

By the time students reach the intermediate grades, they have begun to accept that there is a difference between revising and editing. They have usually begun to take pride in their work, and they want it to be the best that it can be—not just in terms of the way they've punctuated their sentences, but in terms of the way they've told their story or built their essay. They have matured as writers enough to know that their first efforts aren't necessarily their best efforts. As they begin to internalize what constitutes good writing, they learn how to determine which aspects of a composition need improvement. They're able to consider different genres, purposes, and audiences and to grasp that each combination has different characteristics. Naturally, this is especially true if they're receiving good instruction on a variety of techniques and on the revising process as a whole.

And that is where we, as teachers, play an enormously important role. If we guide them well, if we help them at every possible juncture to grasp and respect the nature of good writing, they'll want to take on the challenge of improving their writing. They'll come to understand that revision is as necessary to good writing as the initial draft is. This section presents a set of varied lessons to help you help your students accomplish that goal.

In the revision phase, this student takes a careful look at the way she has developed her ideas and expressed herself and discovers places to improve her story.

Using imagery in writing: focus on similes and metaphors

EXPLANATION: Figures of speech help writers create more concrete visual images for readers. This lesson helps students develop their understanding of figures of speech in two ways. First, it engages them in a listening activity in which they pay focused attention to an expert author's use of imagery. Second, it provides them with a method to home in on figures of speech in their own writing.

Skill Focus

Creating imagery by using adjectives, adverbs, similes, metaphors, sensory details, and concrete examples

Materials & Resources

☆ Passages from published texts that illustrate good use of imagery, especially similes and metaphors (used in this lesson: *Appalachia: The Voices of Sleeping Birds* by Cynthia Rylant)

☆ Transparency showing several paragraphs of published text containing similes and metaphors

Quick Hints

Label a bulletin board "Phrases That Create Pictures in Our Minds" and use it to post quotes students have gathered from published authors.

Preliminary Considerations: *To make your Read Alouds for this lesson especially expressive, you might want to practice at home first. We recommend using Cynthia Rylant's* Appalachia: The Voices of Sleeping Birds *because it is an evocative, poetic book. Read the book aloud to students once before the lesson so they can simply listen to the language and appreciate the beauty of the words. During this first Read Aloud, be sure to point out the remarkable watercolor pictures by Barry Moser.*

STEPS

1. Tell students that this lesson will focus on how writers use imagery to paint pictures in their readers' minds with words. Remind students that authors can employ many different kinds of imagery; in this lesson you'll emphasize figures of speech, especially similes and metaphors. Encourage students to brainstorm other kinds of figures of speech, such as personification and onomatopoeia. Review definitions as needed with the class.

2. Now read aloud Rylant's book a second time. This time ask your students to close their eyes so that they can concentrate more fully on the descriptions. Tell students that, as they listen, they should use the author's words to create their own vivid pictures of the people, animals, and setting of the Appalachian Mountains.

3. Display the prepared transparency of text from the book. Have volunteers come forward to underline the metaphors and similes. Encourage them, as well, to underline other words and phrases that they feel are good illustrations of how Rylant uses words to create images.

4. Tell students you're going to give them a method to create vivid images and to construct their own similes and metaphors. Using a transparency or the chalkboard, write this sentence:

   The cook had double chins, an obvious reflection of the food she loved so much.

   Under the sentence, draw or display a simple chart like the one on page 62. Tell students you're going to use this chart to help you find another way to illustrate how the cook looked. First, you need to pinpoint the characteristics or elements—in this instance, the curved, rounded, or repeated lines that characterize double chins—to be "painted" by your words. Write *curved, rounded, repeated lines* under the "Outstanding characteristics" column heading. Your next step is to brainstorm about anything in your experience that has similarly curved, rounded, and repeated lines. List any images you come up with in the last column.

What you want to describe	Outstanding characteristics	Brainstormed list of other things that possess that characteristic
Cook's double chins	Curved, rounded, repeated lines	—Strands of pearls on a necklace —Clothes hanging on a line —Scalloped icing on a cake —Draped valance

5. Discuss your images with the class. Model using your favorite image in a newly created sentence. For instance:

> The cook's neck lapped like strands of pearls, reflecting the richness of the food she loved so much.

6. Invite students to brainstorm several other items with you. Have them provide distinguishing characteristics and suggest illustrative examples. See below for a sample chart.

What you want to describe	Outstanding characteristics	Brainstormed list of other things that possess that characteristic
An ocean wave	Force, circular motion	—Swing of a blade —Swiping paw of a tiger —Sweeping of a jump rope
Familiar melody	Warmth, comfort	—Aroma of apple pie —Security blanket

7. Have students try this technique in their next composition. Remind them to strive for vivid imagery in all their writing and to look for appropriate places to include it in pieces they are revising.

8. You might also have students create a section in their writing folders exclusively for ideas they've gathered from published authors. Encourage them to include passages that contain figures of speech and to label each figure of speech appropriately. They'll soon become aware of how often their favorite writers employ these techniques.

Using imagery in writing: focus on sensory details and concrete examples

EXPLANATION: This lesson works in tandem with the previous lesson, expanding students' experience of figurative language to nonfiction writing. Here students learn how writers can engage their readers by using sensory images and concrete examples.

Skill Focus

Creating imagery by using adjectives, adverbs, similes, metaphors, sensory details, and concrete examples

Materials & Resources

☆ Textbook or other content material currently being studied

☆ Chart (prepared ahead) of content material that students are currently learning

Quick Hints

Read aloud great authors' works that include sensory details and concrete examples. After reading passages that are particularly powerful, stop and discuss how the specific words the author has chosen help readers to engage their imagination and to become part of the scene.

STEPS

1. Refresh students' understanding of the importance of imagery in writing by reviewing the definitions and discussion in the previous lesson. Tell the class that today's lesson will expand on that one in two ways. First, it will examine how authors use sensory details and concrete examples in addition to figures of speech. Second, it will move from fictional text to nonfiction material. Students may be surprised to learn that nonfiction writers can also greatly enhance the effectiveness of their writing by employing powerful, vivid imagery and language.

2. Display your chart of content material that students are currently learning. For example, in science students might be studying how organisms have developed certain body parts to survive in an ecosystem. A sample chart, displaying facts for this topic, is below.

Type of bird	Feature	How feature helps bird survive in ecosystem
Finch	Beak	For eating seeds, fruit, or insects
Osprey	Talons	For catching and carrying prey
Ostrich	Long legs	For speed

3. Model writing a short paragraph describing a bird from the chart. Include sensory details and concrete examples. A sample paragraph follows. Words that evoke images and/or sensory details are underlined (you might underline these words as you write or have volunteers come forward to identify and underline pertinent words afterward).

> The <u>graceful</u> osprey <u>swooped</u> out of the stormy sky with talons extended <u>like a garden rake</u>. The <u>juicy</u>, <u>shiny</u> worm <u>writhed</u> in the moist mud and appeared to signal the osprey <u>as clearly as a lighthouse beacon bringing in a lost ship</u>.

4. Analyze with the class how the sensory words and concrete examples used in the paragraph deepen and enrich the writing. Challenge students to identify the two similes.

5. Have students choose another item from the chart you have created. Ask them to write an original paragraph, incorporating sensory details and concrete examples. You might also ask them to select one of their own previously written pieces and revise it by adding imagery and figurative language.

Using strong verbs

EXPLANATION: Many student writers think they can liven up their writing by adding numerous adjectives. After analyzing selected authors' works, they may discover that it is the right choice of verb, not adjective, that can make all the difference.

Skill Focus

Choosing strong verbs to make writing more vivid

Materials & Resources

☆ Passages that contain strong verbs from well-written published works (used in this lesson: *Among the Hidden* by Margaret Peterson Haddix; also recommended: *John Henry* by Julius Lester and *Shrek!* by William Steig)

Quick Hints

Ask students to illustrate sentences that contain powerful verbs. Post the illustrations, along with their accompanying verbs. Example: *He tugged harder on the door,* accompanied by a drawing of a boy trying with all his might to open a door.

STEPS

1. Explain to the class that it's easy to fall into the "adjective trap"—that is, to believe that the best way to make writing more interesting is to add adjectives during revision. Tell students that, while the well-chosen adjective certainly has its place in writing, there's a secret to especially lively, engaging writing: the verb. The verb, after all, depicts the action; it tells how the nouns and the subjects move and act. So, in just one word, the right verb can convey a great deal—everything from precisely how a character feels to specifically how an animal moves.

2. On a transparency or the chalkboard, display preselected sentences from well-crafted published works. Examples from Margaret Peterson Haddix's book *Among the Hidden* follow.

   * He saw the first tree <u>shudder</u> and fall far off in the distance.
   * He <u>savored</u> one last moment of feeling warm soil beneath his bare feet.
   * He <u>scrambled</u> up faster than usual, <u>dashing</u> for the door to the back stairs.
   * Matthew <u>slumped</u> in his chair at the table.
   * Luke <u>crouched</u> by the kitchen's side window.
   * A beautiful day <u>unfolded</u> and a mild breeze <u>rustled</u> the grass.
   * Luke's stomach <u>churned</u> as he sat on his perch.
   * Jen <u>stabbed</u> the power button on the computer.
   * He <u>tramped</u> up the stairs.
   * He <u>yanked</u> open the door and <u>punched</u> the button.
   * Jen's dad <u>crashed</u> uselessly into the far wall.

3. From your list, highlight several sentences for a discussion about how the author used a powerful verb instead of a passive or ordinary verb. Examine with students how the specificity of the verb helps readers visualize and feel what is happening in the sentence. A list of ordinary verbs, accompanied by the alternative that the author chose to use instead, is below.

   * move—shudder
   * got up—scrambled up
   * sat—slumped
   * enjoyed—savored
   * running—dashing

4. Continue the activity by having students suggest more ordinary verbs that Haddix chose *not* to use in her writing. For each instance, guide students to see how Haddix's chosen verb conveys a specific image more clearly.

5. Have students select a piece of writing from their writing folders. Direct them to revise it by replacing a few ordinary verbs with stronger verbs so that the piece winds up sounding more vivid and lively. Have volunteers share their revisions with the class.

Adverbs: modifying the good, the bad, and the ugly

EXPLANATION:
Intermediate-grade students have likely had far more instruction in the use of adjectives in their writing to make their writing more vivid than they have had in the use of adverbs for the same purpose. Yet, as this lesson demonstrates, adverbs serve the writer in equally powerful ways. (See also the lesson in Section Three on using adverbs to make comparisons, page 45.)

Skill Focus

Using adverbs to make writing more vivid and/or precise

Materials & Resources

☆ Prepared passage that includes adverbs in all four categories

Quick Hints

Many of us grew up playing with what we called "Tom Swifties": puns that use adverbs. Share some of these with your students for fun, and then invite students to invent their own. Here are two examples to get students started:

"Yikes! The tire just blew!" shouted Tom <u>flatly</u>.

"Would you please pass the sugar?" Tom asked <u>sweetly</u>.

STEPS

1. Review with students the basic definition of an adverb—"a word that modifies, describes, or intensifies a verb, an adjective, or another adverb." On a transparency or the chalkboard, provide examples and descriptions of adverb use:

    <u>Today</u> we are taking a test on adverbs. (The adverb *today* modifies the verb *are taking* by telling *when* the test is happening.)

    Jim told Sam to stand <u>there</u>. (The adverb *there* modifies the verb *stand* by describing *where* Sam was supposed to stand.)

    You'll be <u>quite</u> relieved after the test is over! (The adverb *quite* modifies the adjective *relieved* by telling *how much* the person is relieved.)

    He finished the test on adverbs <u>very</u> <u>quickly</u>. (The adverb *very* modifies the adverb *quickly* by describing *how much*; *quickly* modifies the verb *finished* by describing *how* the test taking occurred.)

2. Further clarify with students that all adverbs, whether they modify a verb, adjective, or another adverb, fall into one of four categories. They describe *time (when)*, *place (where)*, *manner (how)*, or *degree (how much)*. With students, look back through the list of example sentences to make sure they understand the role each adverb plays.

3. Using a transparency or the chalkboard, write the four adverb categories as column headings. Next, display a brief passage that includes numerous adverbs and read it aloud. Help students to find and classify the adverbs. One sample passage, followed by the headings, is below. This passage is admittedly a bit gross, but we think students will love it! Note that the passage shows the adverbs underlined, followed by parenthetical letters to indicate the correct categories. These markings are for your convenience and should not be displayed for students.

All About Flies

(t)
<u>Often</u> when I was young, I heard stories about flies landing and

vomiting on things. Although this frightened me when I was little, I
(t)
<u>later</u> classified this tale as one of the "urban myths" we've all been
                                                                    (m)
told. (Haven't you heard the one about the person scheduled <u>quickly</u>
              (m)
for surgery to remove a <u>mysteriously</u> large growth from his head? He

asked for one more chance to scratch the terrible itch it created—
(d)
<u>only</u> to have a disgusting army of ants come streaming out.) So, I'll
            (d)   (d)   (t)
admit to being <u>somewhat</u> surprised to find <u>only</u> <u>lately</u> that the fly

(d)

story is <u>absolutely</u> true! Flies don't have teeth or tongues to chew

their food. Instead, they vomit and use the enzymes and digestive

juices to liquefy what they want to eat. As if that weren't
(d)

disgusting enough, flies' feet are <u>entirely</u> covered with about 1,500
(d)

taste hairs, making them 10,000 times <u>more</u> sensitive to tastes

than we are!

I guess that's enough disgusting stuff to tell you. I think I'll get
(t)   (p)

busy <u>now</u> and swat some flies before one lands <u>nearby</u>!

TIME	PLACE	MANNER	DEGREE

4. To conclude, remind students that adverbs can make their writing more powerful and can help greatly with developing voice. Do add a warning, however: The adverbs that express degree are often overused. For example, the adjective *beautiful* is descriptive enough; adding the adverb *very* to form *very beautiful* actually adds nothing to the meaning.

Writing appropriately for different audiences

EXPLANATION: When you're writing for a specific audience, you may use varying degrees of formality or informality. The person addressed and the specific reason for the writing determine the format and appropriate word choices. Students make these kinds of decisions naturally in their oral communications. This lesson helps them apply the same distinctions more consciously to their writing.

Skill Focus

Making appropriate word choices for audience and purpose

Materials & Resources

☆ Two pieces of writing, one formal and one informal, on the same topic

Quick Hints

Design a bulletin board for displaying students' original compositions (Step 4). Divide the board in half and label the areas "Formal Writing" and "Informal Writing." Have pairs post their own pieces and explain why they chose one side or the other.

STEPS

1. Ask students to reflect on how their patterns of speaking adjust almost intuitively according to the people they're conversing with. Have them brainstorm characteristics of their typical conversations with friends, siblings, parents, and teachers. How do these different audiences affect what they say and how they say it? Conclude by drawing a comparison to written communication and review with students how writers need to consider their audience when they compose a piece.

2. Choose a topic of particular interest to your class. Model writing a fifth-grade girl's personal letter to a peer and her letter to the editor for the town newspaper about the same topic. Two sample letters follow.

Letter to Peer

Dear Susan,

   WOW!! You won't believe what is happening at River Bend this year! We have to wear uniforms and I am totally against this idea. This weekend my mom and I went clothes shopping and bought the neatest new outfits for school and now I can't wear them. Instead I have to wear navy and khaki shirts and pants! How boring!! Don't you feel sorry for me?

Love ya,

Meg

Letter to the Editor

To the editor:

   River Bend Elementary has just introduced a new dress code. All students must wear a uniform with only navy and khaki colors. Students now have no freedom of choice where clothes are concerned. Some students do not believe that this is a fair policy. As one of those students, I want to voice my strong feeling that we who are most directly affected should be consulted before a change of this significance is implemented.

Meg Allen

5th-Grade Student

3. Read the two examples aloud. Guide the class in analyzing the variety in style and word choice the writer has used for each audience. A sample list of comparisons is below.

Letter to peer: informal / first person

- contractions used
- multiple uses of exclamation mark
- colloquial word choice:
    —*wow*
    —*totally*
    —*neatest*
    —*boring*

Letter to the editor: formal / primarily third person

- well-constructed sentences
- serious tone; no exclamation marks
- carefully chosen vocabulary and word choice:
    —*introduced*
    —*concerned*
    —*policy*
    —*consulted*
    —*significance*
    —*implemented*

4. Introduce a new topic. Have students work in pairs to select an audience and purpose and to write a brief composition. Remind them to choose words and a style appropriate for their targeted audience.

Analyzing published works to understand the concept of length

EXPLANATION: This activity is designed to eliminate the age-old question that students at upper intermediate grades ask every time they put pencil to paper: "How long does it have to be?" Let them discover that it has to be just as long as it takes to say what needs to be said!

Skill Focus

Analyzing published examples as models for writing; understanding how long a piece of writing needs to be

Materials & Resources

☆ One piece of poster board or chart paper for each group

☆ Colored markers

Quick Hints

During independent reading time, ask students to search for and flag examples of well-written text that is particularly concise and to the point. Cut out or photocopy these excerpts and keep them for future use. You may want students to read and reread them in order to develop fluency.

You might also want to post this adage from Henry David Thoreau, which describes good writing and revision: "Not that it need be long, but that it take a long time to make it short."

STEPS

1. Tell students that this lesson is a bit different from their previous writing lessons—they will be constructing bar graphs (so they may even think they're in math class)! Explain that while the graphing should be fun and will certainly involve math skills, the purpose is definitely focused on writing. The bar graphs will represent the length of different compositions. The goal of the lesson is to help students explore and analyze this question: Is there a definitive number of pages or words that a writer must use in a specific genre?

2. Organize the class into small groups and give each group a different genre to explore. You might work with one particular group of students if you feel they would benefit from your direct involvement. Otherwise, move from group to group.

3. Either furnish or have students locate five different samples of the same genre. For instance, for informational text related to one selected topic, you might use a science book, a trade book, an encyclopedia, the Internet, and a magazine article. For fiction (realistic, fantasy/science fiction, or historical), you might use novels and short stories. For poetry, you can supply anthologies and poetry collections by one author.

4. Instruct the groups to calculate the number of words, paragraphs, or pages used. (Any of these calculations will work for this activity, but you'll need to decide ahead of time which you'd like to target. If you want students to figure out the number of words or paragraphs, have students calculate an average per page times the total number of pages for long selections.)

5. Have students set up their bar graphs by listing the genre at the top of the graph, the number of pages or words as the vertical axis, and the names of the selections on the horizontal axis. Direct them to fill in the graphs according to the findings they discover. See the end of this lesson for a completed sample graph.

6. Have each group present their findings to the whole class once the graphs are completed. Display them in your room so that everyone can view all the findings.

7. As you bring closure to this lesson, guide students to answer the question you posed at the start: There is no definitive number of pages or words that a writer must use in any genre. Writers take as many pages or words as necessary to say what needs to be said. Put another way, the issue is fundamentally whether or not the author fulfills his/her purpose with the number of words he/she has chosen. In this vein, you might have the class think about works

they have already read and consider this question: *Why* is that particular poem 100 words and that one only 10 words, this book 100 pages and that one 500?

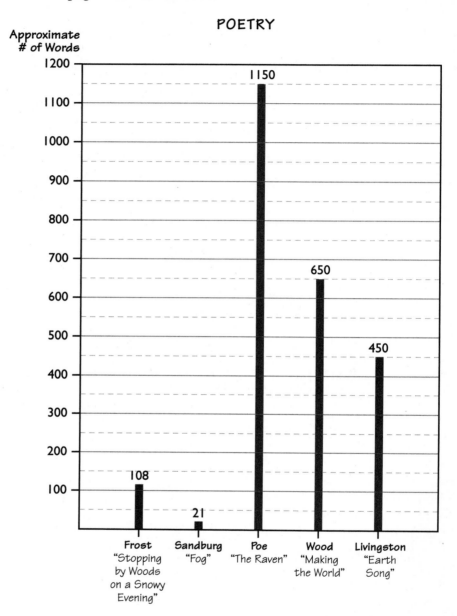

POETRY

Approximate # of Words

1200	
1100	1150 (Poe "The Raven")
1000	
900	
800	
700	650 (Wood)
600	
500	450 (Livingston)
400	
300	
200	
100	108 (Frost), 21 (Sandburg)

Frost "Stopping by Woods on a Snowy Evening"
Sandburg "Fog"
Poe "The Raven"
Wood "Making the World"
Livingston "Earth Song"

Using dialogue to enhance writing

EXPLANATION: Writers use many narrative devices to add depth, life, and voice to their writing. Here students learn about one of the most effective of those devices—dialogue. By observing how one highly regarded author incorporates dialogue, they learn that the same scene can change dramatically when direct speech, rather than static description, is employed. (You might teach this lesson in conjunction with the Section Three lesson on dialogue, page 50.)

Skill Focus

Using a range of narrative devices, such as dialogue

Materials & Resources

☆ Examples of narratives that successfully use dialogue (used in this lesson: *Boy: Tales of Childhood* by Roald Dahl)

Quick Hints

On strips of paper, write situations such as the ones below and put them in a basket. Divide the class into groups of four and ask each group to choose a strip of paper and act out the scenario described. Then have groups write down the dialogue they created.

> Two friends dare you to eat a worm!

> The chorus tryouts are over and you made it!

STEPS

1. Discuss with the class the role that dialogue plays in a piece of writing: It helps place readers right there in a book's action and brings to life the characters behind the words. Tell students that in this lesson they will observe how a favorite children's author, Roald Dahl, uses dialogue to enliven and enrich his writing. In his book *Boy: Tales of Childhood*, Dahl captivates and delights the reader with his boyhood antics, frequently by describing scenes through conversation.

2. Explain that you are going to present the same scene from this book in two different ways. Here is the context for the scene: During a test, Roald asks his friend Dobson if he can borrow a pencil. The headmaster thinks he is cheating.

3. Side by side on a transparency or the chalkboard, write the following two depictions of the scene:

    a. Captain Hardcastle caught me talking to Dobson. The headmaster would not stop talking and accusing me.

    b. Captain Hardcastle (the headmaster) had leapt to his feet and was pointing at me and shouting, "You're talking! I saw you talking! Don't try to deny it! I distinctly saw you talking behind your hand."

4. Read both versions aloud. Ask students to compare the two and answer this question: Which one provides more insight into the character Captain Hardcastle? In a discussion, perhaps using additional examples like the one above, guide students to grasp how narratives come to life when dialogue is incorporated.

5. Have students select a piece of writing from their folders and experiment with improving it by revising some of the scenes to include conversation and dialogue. Be sure to review the appropriate use of quotation marks and commas as part of this activity.

Adding and deleting

EXPLANATION: In this lesson students learn an extremely effective technique for helping one another revise their work. It is a valuable means for having students respond to each other beyond the sharing they normally do in the Writing Workshop. However, because it exposes students to peer criticism, we recommend introducing it only when they seem fairly confident as writers.

Skill Focus

Revising writing for meaning, clarity, and focus by adding and deleting

Materials & Resources

☆ Four small sticky-notes for each student

☆ Students' own previous writing samples

☆ One sample of your previous writing on a transparency

Quick Hints

This same technique can be used to get students to look closely at any number of revisions—deleting words, adding more description, adding sensory details, or anything you've been teaching that you want them to think about applying. Once students are familiar with the technique and comfortable critiquing one another's work, you can offer this as an independent activity.

STEPS

1. Tell students that you're going to need their help to refine a piece of your previous writing. Although just about any piece will do, it's preferable to use one that you consider a bit incomplete. Place it on the overhead projector and read it aloud.

2. Direct students to jot down on one sticky-note something that they would like to know more about in your writing. Tell them to be as specific as possible.

3. After they've had a few minutes to jot down their comments, call on a few volunteers to come forward and share their observations. As each student shares, take the sticky-note and place it close to the point at which you will consider adding the requested information. Thank each student for his or her suggestion and say you'll consider acting on the suggestion.

4. Now ask students to try this among themselves, using a preselected a piece of their own writing. Place them in cooperative groups of four and tell them to pass their papers to the student to their right. Students then read the paper they've received and consider what they'd like to know more about. When they've decided on one item, they write their suggestion on one of their three remaining sticky-notes and place the note at the precise place in the draft where they'd like more information.

5. Then everyone again passes the paper to the right. The second reader reads the new paper, considers something he or she wants to know, writes it on another sticky-note, and places the sticky-note at the appropriate spot on the paper.

6. This process continues until the paper returns to its original owner, who then has three suggestions for things his or her peers want to know more about. The writer studies each comment carefully.

7. Stress to students that whether they actually make the suggested revisions is a personal decision. They need to decide if adding the information will improve the piece. If so, they should engage in revising; if not, they should be ready to explain why their piece is better as is.

8. Repeat this same procedure on another day, but focus this time on suggestions for deleting material.

Revising by combining and rearranging sentences

EXPLANATION: Students have already worked with combining shorter sentences to form longer ones in Section Three, but there the emphasis was on punctuation and parts of speech. In this lesson they also analyze and experiment with interesting, varied sentence structure, but now the emphasis is on experiencing the beauty and flow that more complex sentence structure offers. It's important to use a particularly well-crafted poetic book, such as Cynthia Rylant's *Appalachia: The Voices of Sleeping Birds*, for this lesson.

Skill Focus

Combining and rearranging words, sentences, and paragraphs

Materials & Resources

☆ Especially well-written book (recommended in this lesson: *Appalachia: The Voices of Sleeping Birds* by Cynthia Rylant)

☆ Transparency prepared ahead, displaying text from that book

Quick Hints

Create a notebook for your writing center in which you and your students record well-crafted sentences that you and they have discovered during independent reading. Students can read through these sentences occasionally for inspiration in their writing.

STEPS

1. Tell students that this lesson will provide an opportunity to observe and experience the beauty of well-crafted sentences. Remind them that sentences can flow in unusual and unexpected ways, using clauses, phrases, and connecting words. If you haven't already read aloud Cynthia Rylant's *Appalachia: The Voices of Sleeping Birds* (it was used in the lessons on pages 40 and 61), read it aloud to students and invite them to simply listen carefully and enjoy the language.

2. Display a prepared transparency of a single page on which there are sentences you consider well crafted (just about any page of this book would do!). Here are two sample sentences from page 3:

   Many of them were born in coal camps in tiny houses which stood on poles and on the sides of which you could draw a face with your finger because coal dust had settled on their walls like snow.

   The owners of these dogs grew up more used to trees than sky and inside them had this feeling of mystery about the rest of the world they couldn't see because mountains came up so close to them and blocked their view like a person standing in a doorway.

3. Ask students to analyze each sentence to discover how many short sentences they can find within each more complex and flowing sentence. Possible short sentences for each are listed below:

   For sentence 1:
   - Many of them were born in coal camps.
   - The houses in the camps were tiny.
   - The houses stood on poles.
   - You could draw a face on the side of the house.
   - You could draw the face with your finger.
   - Coal dust had settled on their walls.

   For sentence 2:
   - The people owned dogs.
   - The dogs' owners were more used to trees than to sky.
   - The dogs' owners had a feeling of mystery inside them.
   - The mystery was about the rest of the world.
   - They couldn't see the rest of the world.
   - Mountains blocked their vision of the rest of the world.
   - The mountains came up close to them.
   - The mountains were like a person.

4. Finally, direct students to select a paragraph or brief composition from their writing folders and revise it by combining short, choppy sentences into more interesting sentences.

Expanding and embedding ideas

EXPLANATION: This lesson gives students further practice in moving away from short, choppy sentences and encourages them to create interesting sentences that have more sophisticated structures. We can't stress enough: model, model, model! And then give students plenty of opportunities to experiment with different ways of using modifiers, coordination, and subordination to communicate their ideas.

Skill Focus

Using modifiers, coordination, and subordination to expand and embed ideas

Materials & Resources

☆ Transparency of a composition that demonstrates both choppy and fluid sentence structure

Quick Hints

To provide further practice with coordinating and subordinating phrases and clauses, make available text from a first-grade basal reader, primer, or simple children's book. Challenge students to use what they've learned about coordination and subordination to rewrite the text with fewer sentences that are more sophisticated.

STEPS

1. Review with students the different ways in which they can combine short, choppy sentences to make their writing more flowing and connected. In particular, you may want to review the use of semicolons, subordinate clauses, and prepositional phrases. Tell them that this lesson will give them another chance to try out their sentence revising skills.

2. Display a prepared transparency of a composition you've written that includes several paragraphs of simple, choppy sentences as well as one paragraph of fluid, more complex sentences. Read the piece aloud and challenge students to identify the improved paragraph. Have students analyze the differences in sentence structure between that paragraph and the others. Below is a sample composition. (In this model, the final paragraph demonstrates more complex sentence structure.)

Fashion Hurts

Sometimes I think our fashions are absurd. Women today wear shoes with sharp, pointed toes. The shoes have tall thin heels. It's like walking on a tightrope. Men wear a long piece of cloth. The cloth is in bright colors. It is wrapped around their necks. It is called a tie. It serves no purpose whatsoever. Some boys wear pants hanging far down on their hips. They literally have to hold onto them. Otherwise, they would lose them. Many girls spend endless hours on their hair. They curl their hair. They iron it. They color it. They perm their hair. All of this is done to fit the popular styles of the day.

Our fashions today are silly. But I know there have been more absurd fashions in history. Fashion was extremely painful for girls in China. This was several centuries ago. They defined beauty as having tiny feet. They bound the feet of little girls. They wrapped them tighter and tighter every day. The bones in the feet finally broke. The feet were bent back. They were folded and tucked into an upside-down V. By this time, the feet measured just over three inches!

How did the Chinese women walk on these deformed feet? They didn't. These women usually had rich husbands. Servants waited on them. They could only sit all day. This occurred from the tenth century until 1911. It was finally banned!

Now that I really think about it, I'm realizing that things aren't so bad today after all. Pointed shoes may not be practical, but at least women can walk in them. And men's ties are merely ornamental; at least they don't hurt. It's okay to spend time on our hair since that doesn't hurt either. Aren't we glad we didn't live in China several hundred years ago when fashion really did hurt?

You might further experiment with the many ways to craft a sentence. Give students a few simple sentences and let them see how many ways they can rewrite and combine them without changing the meaning. Below is a model you might use.

Short, choppy sentences: First, we are going to lunch. Then we are going to read another chapter of our novel. The name of the novel is *Frindle*.

Possible longer sentences, each of which combines the meaning of the three short sentences:

- First, we are going to lunch, and then we're going to read another chapter of our novel *Frindle*.

- After lunch, we're going to read another chapter of our novel *Frindle*.

- We're going to read another chapter of our novel *Frindle* after we go to lunch.

- Reading our novel *Frindle* is what we'll do after we have lunch.

3. Now invite volunteers to help you rework the composition. Encourage students to embed, coordinate, and subordinate phrases, words, and ideas so that the composition flows more smoothly. Review that coordination usually involves connecting equally important clauses; subordination means connecting clauses that aren't equal in emphasis. Embedding refers to interjecting words and phrases into a sentence. Make use of proofreader symbols as you do the revising to demonstrate the process for students.

Writing in a Variety of Forms

One of the greatest challenges we have in the classroom—probably in all of education—is to convince students that what we have to teach them is worth their time and effort. A curriculum of facts and figures to memorize won't convince them. A curriculum that involves writing won't necessarily make the difference. But a curriculum that asks students to write for genuine purposes and audiences at least has a real chance. As respected educator and author Lucy Calkins (1991) put it: "Writing is lifework, not deskwork." We know that not all writing is lifework, but as teachers we can make sure that much of what students write in our classrooms is related to real-life purposes and real-world audiences. Because it relates to their own lives, that kind of writing will go a long way toward convincing them that what they do in the classroom really is worth the effort.

Writing shouldn't be taught as an end unto itself. It needs to be presented as the means to an end. Students need to see the power of writing and what it can accomplish. Writing expert Ralph Fletcher (1993) put it best: "You don't learn to write by going through a series of preset exercises. You learn to write by grappling with a real subject that truly matters to you."

So, what truly matters to fourth, fifth, and sixth graders? Here is just a sampling of what we've found in our many years of experience. For these grades, real purpose might involve

☆ writing e-mail messages or "snail mail" letters to friends,

☆ composing persuasive letters that have a potential impact on the real world,

☆ generating plays or productions that will be shared with audiences,

☆ producing class newspapers that will inform peers and parents of what's happening in the classroom.

To accomplish the task of helping students experience this kind of meaningful writing, we must teach and model how writing changes according to form, purpose, and audience. Students need to learn that many elements of writing—for example, word choice, voice, development, sentence structure, and degree of formality—change according to form, purpose, and audience. There is a vast difference between a friendly letter and a newspaper article and between a free verse poem and an expository composition. It is our job as teachers to help students grasp these differences.

There is another important reason to provide real purposes and audiences for students who are learning to write. That reason, quite simply, is that there is power in writing. Students need to discover firsthand that writing can get results. It can anger or soothe the reader; it can get someone a job; it can bring great pleasure to an audience; it can help the writer gain new understanding about his or her own personal life as well as about the surrounding world. Writing can open all these portals and so many more, and students in the intermediate grades are ready and able to experience the riches that writing can provide. It's our job as teachers to give them these opportunities.

Let's take a look now at a number of lessons that will motivate your students as they discover the power of writing.

March 28,

Dear mom and dad,
I think that we need to get a pet. My opinion is that we get a Miniature Bulldog. I will tell you why I think I should be able to get a pet.

One of the reasons I think I should get a Miniature Bulldog is because they're very small. That means they won't take up so much space. Another reason we need a Miniature Bulldog is because I'm getting older and I'm more responsible. That means you won't have to do all the work. Another reason is they are not mean. So that means it won't bite when you tell it to do something. Another reason I should be able to have a Miniature Bulldog is that I can get outside and not bug you saying that I'm bored because I would have a dog. That's the reasons we should get a Miniature Bulldog.

In conclusion, mom and dad, I have worked very hard and I know that if you think about it you will make the right choice.

Love,
Your Daughter,
Kelcy

P.S. I'll love you forever!

Advice from a Carrot

"Eat your vegetables,"
my mother said.
"They're good for you."
There were a million and three things
I wanted to do to those vegetables,
like mash them with a hammer
or feed them to the dog,
ubt eating them was not one of the things.
I said to the carrot that lay on my plate,
"Why must you taste the way you do,
and not the way chocolate cake does?"
The carrot spoke back to me,
"I'm not sure. But why must you eat me?
I'd rather be outside playing with
My friend, Cabbage."
"Very well," I said,
and I grabbed the carrot and
threw it hard as I could out the window.
There, I thought,
That's one less carrot.

Students' writing can take so many interesting forms. Here are two delightful examples: one student's persuasive letter to her parents and another's free verse poem.

Writing patterned poems in response to reading

Skill Focus

Writing in response to what is read and written; writing original patterned poems (bio-poems)

Materials & Resources

☆ Nonfiction book and/or work of fiction (used in this lesson: *More Than Anything Else* by Marie Bradby)

☆ Brainstorming chart for bio-poem (See Appendix, page 118)

Quick Hints

To increase students' excitement about writing original poetry, consider helping them publish it. For example, see if you can post students' poems on your school Web site. The following websites provide outlets for publishing children's writing:

www.stonesoup.com
www.writingconference.com
www.merlynspen.org

STEPS

1. Tell students that in this lesson they will learn about an effective way (that is also a lot of fun) to express and convey their knowledge about a special person or character. The person could be a historical figure (as in this lesson) or a fictional character, perhaps even an animal. The format they will use for their original writing is the bio-poem.

2. Start by brainstorming the person/character's feelings, experiences, characteristics, and background setting. In this lesson we focus on Booker T. Washington (using information from *More Than Anything Else* by Marie Bradby). The chart below provides a model for the brainstorming activity:

BOOKER T. WASHINGTON			
Feelings	**Actions**	**Description**	**Setting**
• Wanted to learn to read • Always hungry • Imagines reading the black marks on paper • Dreams of being the best reader • Hungry for reading • Tries to jump without legs • Feels dreams slipping away • Feels like he has jumped into another world and he is saved • Feels like he can hold the picture of his name forever	• Packs salt in barrels • Cuts hands, arms, legs, and soles of feet with salt crystals • Catches frogs • Listens to coal miners' tales • Receives a blue alphabet book from his mother • Stares at marks • Draws marks on dirt floor • Looks for newspaperman • Jumps up and down like when he was baptized in the creek • Lingers over picture of his name drawn in the dirt	• Nine-year-old African-American boy • Son of salt worker • Tired arms • Hard worker • Legs stained with salt	• Malden, West Virginia • Fall of 1865 • Saltworks

2. Model for students the structure of a bio-poem. Below is a line-by-line description and a sample bio-poem based on the brainstormed information about Booker T. Washington.

Line 1   Begin with first name of the character
Line 2   4 words to describe a relationship
Line 3   "Lover of" (list 3 items)
Line 4   "Who feels" (list 3 items)
Line 5   "Who fears" (list 3 items)
Line 6   "Who would like to" (list 3 items)

Line 7   "Resident of" (state setting)
Line 8   End with last name of the character

BOOKER T.

Son of salt worker

Lover of books, reading, the newspaperman

Who feels a desire to learn, eager to jump without legs, joy upon reading his name

Who fears dreams slipping away, not finding the newspaperman, cutting his feet with salt crystals

Who would like to be the best reader, jump into another world, hold the picture of his name forever

Resident of West Virginia

WASHINGTON

4. Finally, invite students to write their own bio-poems based on content you are studying or a favorite novel, employing the process you have modeled.

Employing different ways to communicate ideas

EXPLANATION: So often we find ourselves saying to students, "If you have time left over, you could illustrate what you've written." In this lesson we focus on visual literacy itself, exploring the role pictures can play in communicating ideas. Many times they truly are worth a thousand words. Here we give students permission to use and further develop their visual communication skills.

STEPS

1. Remind students that a given set of information can be presented in many different ways. In this lesson they'll have the opportunity to consider a range of visual—as well as verbal—communication possibilities.

2. Tell students that you will try to convey the same factual information to them by two very different means. Using a prepared transparency, display both a graphic illustration and a written description of the same facts. Read aloud the passage and walk through the visual. A sample visual—the food pyramid—and a passage about the food pyramid follow.

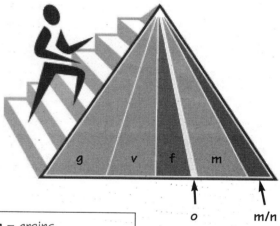

KEY: **g** = grains
v = vegetables
f = fruits
o = oils
m = milk products
m/n = meats and nuts

A Pyramid for Health

The U.S. Department of Agriculture has given us some guidelines for healthier lifestyles and eating choices. We all need a sufficient amount of exercise daily. Each food group should make up a portion of our diet. Grains should make up the greatest portion of our diet. We should eat vegetables and milk products in equal amounts. We should also eat fruits every day—a little less than the vegetables and milk products. Meats and nuts are necessary because they have protein, but we shouldn't eat too much protein. We should consume oils but only in very small amounts because they have lots of calories. So, to conclude, we need to balance our diets according to these particular guidelines and get daily exercise to live healthy lives.

Skill Focus

Writing informational pieces; summarizing and organizing ideas from multiple sources using charts, graphs, outlines, and lists

Materials & Resources

☆ Transparency of graphic of the federal food pyramid (see Step 2 or download from www.pueblo.gsa.gov/cic_text/food/food-pyramid/main.htm or a similar site)

☆ Blank transparencies (one for each small group)

☆ Transparency pens

☆ Index cards prepared ahead of class, each listing a topic and possible formats for conveying information

☆ Resources for research

Quick Hints

To encourage students to use their artistic talents to illustrate their writing and to present and convey their ideas visually, keep various tools in your classroom publishing center or writing center. A few basics include colored markers, colored pencils, sketch pads, watercolors, and charcoal pencils.

3. Now ask students which format they think is most effective in communicating the food guidelines. Have them debate the pluses and minuses of the two approaches.

4. After a brief discussion, organize students into small groups. Have each group choose an index card (see Materials & Resources). Each group is to use resources you've made available to them to prepare a transparency that includes both a written and a visual interpretation of the selected topic. When the transparencies are complete, invite groups to share them with the whole class. A few possible topics and suggested formats are below.

Diagram of the parts of the eyeball	Describe parts of the eyeball with words
Pie graph of current energy sources	Explain with words different energy sources
Map of routes of Marco Polo	Description of the routes
Time line of European settlement in America	Explain in text the chronology of European settlement
Flow chart of government checks and balances	Explain in words the system of checks and balances

Writing summaries

EXPLANATION: Summary writing can be difficult for young writers. Many students want to include everything in a summary; they find it difficult to sift through a passage to find the big ideas. But with well-planned and targeted direct instruction and practice in writing summaries, most students will improve their skills dramatically.

Skill Focus

Writing summaries of reading selections to include main ideas and significant details

Materials & Resources

☆ *Dirty, Rotten, Dead?* by Jerry Emory

☆ Transparency of Summarizing Organizer (See Appendix, page 120)

Quick Hints

Challenge students to write summaries of textbook chapters. Guide them to focus on the headings and subheadings and to include these elements in the summary. Often students ignore these important text features, but they are potentially a great aid: After all, authors include them to point out what is important.

STEPS

1. Review with students the basic elements of a summary. It is a concise composition that sums up the gist of a body of information. A summary must include the main idea and the most important—not simply the most interesting—facts. Tell students that in this lesson they will have the opportunity to summarize material from a detailed, descriptive essay. Their job will be to use an organizer to sort out the key concepts and then write a summary of the information.

2. Using a transparency or the chalkboard, display or write a preselected passage. A sample from *Dirty, Rotten, Dead?* follows. (Admittedly, this passage is a bit gross, but students should love it!)

What's That Smell?

The very things that help animals (and people) live also cause them to rot and stink when they die. Intestinal bacteria, stomach acids, and enzymes help live animals digest their food. When an animal dies, these things keep on digesting, but now they eat away at the dead body from inside.

Intestinal bacteria create foul-smelling gas as they decompose the rotting body. This putrid gas also causes some dead animals to bloat (inflate like a balloon). The gas combines with rotting body parts and decayed blood to form two chemicals that add to the smell: putrescine and cadaverine.

3. Display your transparency of the Summarizing Organizer. Discuss the column titles: How may what's interesting differ from what's important? Stress that while it's important to fill out both columns in order to sort and sift the information, only the information in the right-hand column will become the basis of students' summary. Work through the two processes (note taking and summarizing) with the class. Underline key words or important ideas to help students see the "big picture."

4. With students' help, fill in the organizer with appropriate words, phrases, and ideas from the passage. At this point it helps to draw a large X over the "What's Interesting" column so students understand that this material is not to be used in the summary. Finally, model how you combine key words and ideas to construct new sentences. (Be sure to stress this step; otherwise, many students will copy directly from the original passage.) A completed sample organizer follows.

Name _____   Date _____

WHAT'S INTERESTING (Include small details in this column.)	WHAT'S IMPORTANT (Include main ideas and key details in this column.)
—decaying animals and people stink	intestinal bacteria, acids, and enzymes
—bloating looks like an inflating balloon	—aid in food digestion
—putrescine and cadaverine are names	—eat from inside
of chemicals	—smelly gas created and animals bloat
	rotting body parts and decayed blood
	—form chemicals that smell

SUMMARY OF WHAT WAS READ

Intestinal bacteria, acids, and enzymes help in an animal's or person's digestion but eat away the body from the inside after death. Some dead animals bloat from the smelly gas that results. Rotting body parts and decaying blood form chemicals that add to the smell.

Writing a friendly letter

STEPS

1. Review the parts of a friendly letter with students. These usually include the date, salutation, body, and closing. Tell students that in this lesson they will have an unusual opportunity—they will not only practice writing a friendly letter but they will do so by imagining that they are writing from the perspective of a person in another historical period.

2. Discuss the content facts that students will be using as the basis for their letters. In this lesson, we use facts about human migration in American history. A skeletal set of these facts is described below. For the actual letter, you would use a full unit or chapter of material, far more than is presented here. (Note: A very similar set of facts, although in different format, was also used in the lesson on logical order, page 24.)

> After the Revolutionary War, Americans believed that they had rights to all the land on the continent. Many settlers moved into Texas, which was owned by Mexico. After defeating the Mexicans, Sam Houston declared Texas an independent republic.
>
> The Mormons moved west into Utah, which then belonged to Mexico. The United States and Mexico went to war over borderlines. The U.S. won the war by conquering Mexican forces in New Mexico, California, and Mexico City. Under the terms of a peace treaty, the U.S. bought CA, NV, UT, AZ, NM, CO, and WY from Mexico.
>
> Also during this growth period of the United States, pioneers chose to settle in the Oregon country. Thousands of these travelers used the route known as the Oregon Trail to go westward.
>
> About the same time, gold was discovered in California. In 1849 more than 80,000 gold seekers followed the Oregon Trail, then turned south to California, where they hoped to strike it rich.

3. Model how you select one of the migration events to write about. Using a transparency or the chalkboard, write a friendly letter from the perspective of a pioneer to a relative you left behind. Your letter should demonstrate how you have taken on the role of a member of a family involved in the movement. A sample letter is on page 85.

EXPLANATION: The ability to write a friendly letter is a lifetime skill. Here we ask students to take on the role of a person from a previous era and write a friendly letter as if they lived then. Thus, they gain the chance both to practice their letter writing skills and to immerse themselves, in a personal way, in a particular historical period.

Skill Focus

Writing a friendly letter

Materials & Resources

☆ Facts from historical periods

☆ Sample friendly letter

Quick Hints

Provide the following pointers about friendly letter writing (you might want to create a classroom chart of them):

- Be yourself. Use your own writing voice.
- Share news and interesting information.
- Show an interest in your reader by asking questions. (This is a good way to encourage a return letter, too!)
- Read back over the letter checking for correct content and looking for errors in grammar, punctuation, and spelling.
- Make sure writing is legible.

To provide further models of friendly letters for students, make available *Letters to Children* by C.S. Lewis.

You might want to bind the class's letters together with a titled cover such as "United States Migrations" or "Expansion Memories."

March 20, 1844

Dear Aunt Mary,

It has been so long since I have written you. Mama and Papa keep me so busy while we make the long journey to Texas. The trail is rocky and very dry, but we are getting close to where we will settle. We will have more land than we had in Tennessee, and there will be more job opportunities. Papa heard that we will have to pay more taxes when we arrive. He hopes to find a good job, and I am now old enough to help with the chores if he has to work more. Yesterday Papa talked to a settler about news coming from the West. People are saying that the war may end and Texas may become a state. I would really like that. Would you and Uncle Thomas come to live with us? I hope so! Maybe you can write and tell me what my friends in Tennessee are doing!

Your niece,

Rebecca

4. Finally, have students select one migration event and write an original friendly letter. Help them to follow the model you have provided and call their attention to the pointers included in Quick Hints, which might be displayed on a classroom chart.

Organizing and writing a persuasive piece

EXPLANATION: Most students are quick to offer opinions about many topics, but opinions must be supported by facts and reasons to be persuasive. Here students have the opportunity to organize their thinking about a controversial, real-life issue and then to write a brief persuasive paragraph. We concur with Vacca and Vacca (1986, 2004) that "graphic materials enhance understanding and interpretation"; a graphic organizer to aid students in synthesizing the information for their persuasive writing is central to this lesson.

Skill Focus

Using a graphic organizer to plan writing; writing persuasive pieces following simple patterns

Materials & Resources

☆ Facts and other background as basis for a persuasive piece

☆ Transparency and photocopies, one for each student, of Persuasive Writing Flow Chart (see Appendix, page 121)

Quick Hints

Have students search through magazines and newspapers for examples of persuasive writing. Direct them to pay special attention to the way the writers have structured their pieces.

STEPS

1. Tell students that in this lesson they will have the opportunity to write a persuasive paragraph about a real-life situation. Remind them that the purpose of persuasive writing is to express a strong personal opinion that is aimed at influencing other people's views.

2. On a transparency or the chalkboard, share the following headline and information with students:

   Plan to Require Youths to Have Adult Escorts on Weekend Nights May Reduce Mall Crime Rate

   Facts:
   * For a year crowds of unruly teenagers have exhibited inappropriate behaviors.
   * Loud groups of teens have trashed stores and vehicles.
   * Workload of mall employees has increased.
   * Teens have been caught shoplifting.
   * Plan applies to those 17 years of age and under.
   * Plan would go into effect after 5 p.m. each day.

   Pros (if plan implemented):
   * Calls to police will drop dramatically.
   * Mall will see sales performance improve.
   * Mall will return to a family-friendly environment.
   * Mall will be much quieter.

   Cons (if plan implemented):
   * Some parents will not like the added responsibility of having to accompany their kids to the mall.
   * Kids without parent escorts will not be able to shop or see their friends.
   * Teenagers might trash other places outside the mall.
   * All kids will be affected, not just those who caused the trouble.

3. Hold a brief class discussion about the subject. Explain that the pros and cons presented here are just a sampling of the possibilities. Encourage students to come up with others and to choose a position regarding the headline.

4. Display a transparency of the Persuasive Writing Flow Chart graphic organizer (Appendix, page 121). Discuss the format with the class and explain how it can help students organize and clarify their argument.

5. Distribute a photocopy of the organizer to each student. Direct each student to complete his or her own organizer and then to use it to write a brief persuasive paragraph. Urge them to write as if their piece were to be published on the op-ed page of the local newspaper.

Two-Part Lesson: Planning and Writing an Expository Composition

Part 1: **Planning the composition**

EXPLANATION: This lesson offers students further review and practice in the essential skill of structuring an informational essay (originally discussed in Section Two, pages 32–34). Here students gain experience in writing about historical events. In this first part of the lesson, they use a graphic organizer to plan a well-structured composition.

Skill Focus

Planning and writing pieces with multiple paragraphs

Materials & Resources

☆ Relevant content facts and information

☆ Expository Writing Flow Chart (see Appendix, page 122)

Quick Hints

Use the following checklist to create a classroom display chart:

Checklist for a Well-Written Informational Piece

● Has a clear beginning with topic sentence
● Contains logically organized information
● Includes interesting description, details, and facts
● Includes an ending that summarizes

STEPS

1. Review with students the elements of a good informational (expository) composition. Remind them that it includes an introduction with a topic sentence, at least three supporting (subtopic) paragraphs with details, and a concluding paragraph that summarizes the main point.

2. Tell students that in this multipart lesson they will have the opportunity to first plan and organize and then write an original composition based on historical facts. Review with students the content they will be using as the basis for their compositions. In this lesson, we focus on the influence of rivers on the development of the United States. Discuss historical facts such as the following:

1620s: All settlements in the New England Colonies were located near the ocean or along a river for trade, fishing, etc. The Middle Colonies were settled along the Hudson River.

1632: Maryland was settled near the Potomac River, where trade, rich soil, and fishing were abundant.

1663: Charleston, South Carolina, was settled on the Atlantic Ocean and near rivers, making the city an important seaport. Plantations were built near waterways to transport goods easily and quickly.

1673: France sent an expedition led by Jacques Marquette and Louis Joliet to find and explore the Mississippi River. Many towns and cities were developed along the big river's banks and tributaries (rivers that fed into it). There were few roads; therefore, the rivers were used for travel and trade.

1773: Savannah, Georgia, was built upstream from the mouth of the Savannah River.

1777: During the Revolutionary War, the Americans defeated the British at Saratoga, New York. This great victory gave the Americans control over the Hudson River, a major supply route. This battle was a turning point because it led France to join sides with the Americans.

1781: The Americans and the French attacked the British by land at Yorktown, Virginia, on the Chesapeake Bay. The French fleet blocked British ships from bringing in soldiers and supplies. The British were trapped in Yorktown and forced to surrender.

1790: The Mississippi River became the nation's new western border. During the Industrial Revolution, machines in the cotton mills ran on waterpower; therefore, the mills were built next to rivers. The Erie Canal connected the Atlantic Ocean to Lake Erie and provided shipping routes.

1802: The Spanish closed the port of New Orleans to western farmers. They could no longer use the Mississippi River and the Gulf of Mexico to move their crops and animals to markets in the East and Europe. This prompted the 1803 Louisiana Purchase, which doubled the size of the United States overnight.

1863: During the Civil War, the Union cut off all supplies to Vicksburg, Mississippi. The starving people there were forced to surrender. This victory gave the Union control of the Mississippi River, thus weakening the Confederacy by cutting it into two parts.

3. Model for students how you plan and organize your own composition. Explain that it's important to map out the major segments ahead of time. On a transparency, present the Expository Writing Flow Chart, thinking aloud as you fill in the key sections (see Appendix, page 122). A sample completed organizer follows.

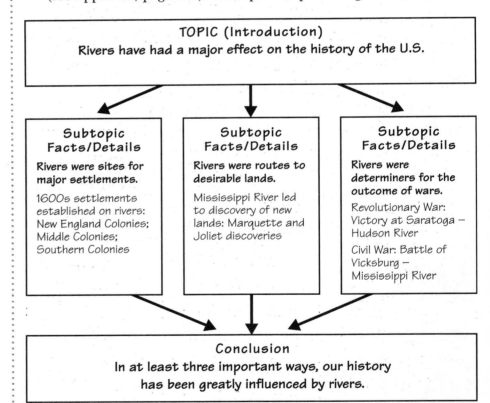

TOPIC (Introduction)
Rivers have had a major effect on the history of the U.S.

Subtopic Facts/Details	Subtopic Facts/Details	Subtopic Facts/Details
Rivers were sites for major settlements.	**Rivers were routes to desirable lands.**	**Rivers were determiners for the outcome of wars.**
1600s settlements established on rivers: New England Colonies; Middle Colonies; Southern Colonies	Mississippi River led to discovery of new lands: Marquette and Joliet discoveries	Revolutionary War: Victory at Saratoga – Hudson River Civil War: Battle of Vicksburg – Mississippi River

Conclusion
In at least three important ways, our history has been greatly influenced by rivers.

4. Distribute a photocopy of the organizer to each student or to pairs of students. Direct students to select a different topic from a social studies unit you have studied or are studying. Following your model, they should identify a topic, list key facts, and fill in their organizers.

Two-Part Lesson: Planning and Writing an Expository Composition

Part 2: Writing the composition

EXPLANATION: This lesson offers students further review and practice in the essential skill of structuring an informational essay (originally discussed in Section Two, pages 32–34). Here students gain experience in writing about historical events. In this second part of the lesson, students write original compositions based on their previous planning.

Skill Focus

Planning and writing pieces with multiple paragraphs

Materials & Resources

☆ Filled-in Expository Writing Flow Charts from Part 1 of this lesson

Quick Hints

Challenge students to create several additional five-paragraph essays on closely related subjects within their overarching topic. These essays can be joined to form a report, which can be stapled together with an illustrated cover. Alternatively, the report can be published on a file folder. Students can illustrate the outside of the folder and staple the report to the inside.

STEPS

1. Review the Expository Writing Flow Chart that you created with the class in Part 1 of this lesson. Using this completed organizer as a guide, model how you write an effective, well-structured composition. Think aloud about the components. A sample piece follows.

The Effect of Rivers on the History of the United States

Because rivers have been sites for settlements, routes to the most desirable new lands, and points of contention in wars, they have had a major effect on the history of the United States.

In the 1600s the New England Colonies, the Middle Colonies, and the Southern Colonies were all established along rivers. The rivers allowed for the development of trading posts, as well as access to a mode of swifter transportation for the settlers.

In 1673, France sent Marquette and Joliet to find and follow the Mississippi River. Trade and settlements quickly grew along the "big river." It became our new western border.

The American victory at Saratoga, New York, on the Hudson River was a turning point in the Revolutionary War, causing France to side with the United States against England. The French aided the Americans by defeating the British in a naval battle near Chesapeake Bay in 1781, thus blocking supply lines to inland troops. During the Civil War, the Union gained control of the Mississippi River at the Battle of Vicksburg. This weakened the Confederacy by cutting it into two parts and led to its defeat.

In at least three important ways, our history has been greatly affected by rivers. To gain real understanding of the way our country developed, we must acknowledge their historical significance.

2. Once you are sure that students understand how you used the content facts and your organizer to create this five-paragraph essay, direct them to take out their own organizers from Part 1 of this lesson. Have students write complete compositions based on their plans, following your model.

Two-Part Lesson: Writing News Articles

Part 1: Learning the format and characteristics of news articles

EXPLANATION: News articles represent a unique, unembellished kind of writing; studying them can help students pare down and focus their own writing. In the first of this two-part lesson, students review news article characteristics and then use those criteria to evaluate published articles.

Skill Focus

Identifying characteristics of news writing

Materials & Resources

☆ 4–5 news articles that will be of interest to students (a different article for each group, with an individual photocopy for each student in the group)

Quick Hints

Clip news articles of interest to display in your writing center and/or on a bulletin board. Encourage students to peruse these periodically as a source of inspiration for their own writing. Invite them to either further research the topics and write informational pieces or adapt the topics for fictional pieces.

STEPS

1. Tell students that they'll soon become reporters, and you want them to become familiar with the way news articles are written. Forewarn them that they'll have an assignment to complete, some research to do, and deadlines—just like real journalists!

2. Review the characteristics of a news article with students. Elicit and record what the class already knows. Add to the list as necessary so that all essential ingredients are included. A sample list follows.

   Most news articles
   * answer the "5 Ws" (*Who, What, Why, When, Where*), usually at the beginning,
   * provide the most important information first and the least important details near the end,
   * are written for the purpose of informing readers,
   * are concise (no unnecessary words),
   * include facts rather than the writer's opinions,
   * have an objective, third-person point of view.

3. Organize the class into four or five small groups. Distribute a different news article to each group. Give the groups about ten minutes to read and discuss their article. Direct students to look for the qualities listed on the display chart, especially the 5 Ws and to be ready to discuss the article with the whole class.

4. Call on each group to share with the class the 5 Ws they have identified in the article. Pose a different question to each group. For instance, you might ask, "What kind of details were included beyond the 5 Ws?" or "Did you find any of the writer's opinions in your article? If not, were opinions of others included? If so, how was that done?"

Two-Part Lesson: Writing News Articles

Part 2: **Writing original news articles**

EXPLANATION: This lesson continues instruction of our exploration of news articles. Here students get a chance to write their own articles. Because the articles will be written as contemporary accounts of historical events or observations of scientific phenomena, this assignment also gives students an opportunity to think about their content knowledge from a whole different perspective as they experience it firsthand.

Skill Focus

Writing news articles

Materials & Resources

☆ Sample news article, based on current content area study

☆ List of criteria from Part 1 of this lesson

☆ Headlines for assignments for student articles

Quick Hints

Invite students to use their reporting skills to create a newspaper for the classroom in which they report their own news—what's being studied, personal accomplishments, new students in school, past and future activities. Parents will surely appreciate and benefit from this update! (See page 100 for an example of a well-done class newsletter.)

STEPS

1. Provide a quick review of the points about news reporting from Part 1 of this lesson.

2. Tell students that they'll be given their writing assignments as reporters today. The assignments will be a bit different from the usual news they read in the paper: Students will be doing on-the-spot reporting about something in history or science that they've studied recently. Using a transparency or the chalkboard, present a model for students. You might either write a sample news article based on a current unit of study in your own classroom or use the following example, which is based on a study of Britain and its colonies:

Sons of Liberty Lead Violent Protests

A group calling itself the Sons of Liberty has protested the recent Stamp Act in a number of ways over the past week, striking out against tax collectors. The group attacked tax collectors in their homes, breaking windows and stealing property. In some instances, the collectors were severely beaten.

Sons of Liberty groups have formed in each of the thirteen colonies in response to the Stamp Act imposed by King George III and the British Parliament. These groups have been advocating the freedom of colonists to make their own laws. They started by urging colonists to boycott British goods, but recent activities have turned violent.

In a recent meeting with British lawmakers, Benjamin Franklin, a representative from Pennsylvania, warned the lawmakers that "the seeds of liberty are universally sown there [in Pennsylvania], and nothing can eradicate them." British leaders did not listen to Franklin's warnings and violence has ensued.

3. Using the criteria you listed in Part 1 of the lesson, have students work with you to review your model article. Turn each of the characteristics into a question. For instance, ask: "Does this article include the 5 Ws (*Who, What, Why, When, Where*) at the beginning?", "Does it provide the most important information first?", and so on. Based on the criteria and the class discussion, make any changes that would improve the article.

4. Finally, give students their assignments. Have them use the criteria and the models to write their own news articles. Listed on page 92 are sample assignments, first from a unit on Britain and its colonies and next from a unit on the systems of the human body.

UNIT: BRITAIN AND ITS COLONIES
Headlines for Assignments (reporters are colonists):

- ☆ Stamp Act Imposed—Boycotts Urged
- ☆ Continental Congress Responds to Taxation
- ☆ Boston Holds Massive Tea Party
- ☆ Loyalists Cry "Treason!"
- ☆ Fighting Breaks Out in Lexington and Concord

UNIT: HUMAN BODY SYSTEMS
Headlines for Assignments (reporters are body parts):

- ☆ Clot Formed in Artery Blamed on Poor Habits
- ☆ Poor Air Quality Affecting Respiratory System
- ☆ Heart Demands More Exercise
- ☆ Bile Plays Major Role in Digestion

Two-Part Lesson: Free Verse Poetry

Part 1: Learning the format and characteristics of free verse poetry

EXPLANATION: Free verse poetry allows those students who resist (or ignore!) the use of conventions in their writing to express themselves with abandon. In the first part of this two-part lesson, students analyze the characteristics of free verse poetry, especially to distinguish it from prose.

Skill Focus

Writing free verse poems

Materials & Resources

☆ 4–5 free verse poems (a different poem for each group)

☆ Resources such as: *Love That Dog* by Sharon Creech; *You Have to Write* by Janet S. Wong; *A Pocketful of Poems* by Nikki Grimes; *Dark Sons* by Nikki Grimes

Quick Hints

Share Sharon Creech's wonderful book *Love That Dog*, as a Read Aloud during your study of poetry. The book is a series of diary entries by a boy who reveals that he hates poetry and doesn't understand why his teacher expects his class to listen to it and even to write it. He soon discovers his own poetic voice— and that, yes, boys can like and write poetry! An extra plus: As the boy's class studies poetry, Creech includes some excellent poems by noted authors.

STEPS

1. Tell students that today they will explore a kind of poetry that may be unfamiliar. Explain that you know how much experience they have had with rhymed and patterned poetry (most primary grades stress this kind of poetry). You hope they'll be pleased to discover a new form of expression called free verse poetry.

2. Comment that in some ways free verse poetry has more in common with prose than with rhymed poetry. However, it is definitely *not* prose, and students' job now is to identify just how it is different. Organize students into small groups. Give each group its own preselected free verse poem to explore for about six to eight minutes. Instruct groups to make a list of all the ways in which they find this poetry to differ from a passage of conventional prose. Tell them to be prepared to present their findings to the class.

3. Bring the class together and ask each group to share one item from their list. Instruct other groups to listen carefully and to check off each item that they, too, have listed. Using a transparency or the chalkboard, make a master list of these observations. Continue until all points have been shared. Add to the list as necessary so that all essential characteristics of free verse poetry are included. A sample list follows.

Free Verse Poetry (as Compared to Prose)

- Punctuation is often abandoned or used sparingly.
- Lines vary in length, but most are much shorter than in prose.
- There's often more white space on the page than in prose.
- It's concise. (A poet whittles until there's nothing else to whittle away.)
- Every word is carefully chosen and contributes to the meaning.

4. Make a classroom display chart of this list for students' ongoing reference during subsequent poetry exploration.

Two-Part Lesson: Free Verse Poetry

Part 2: **Learning how to write a free verse poem**

EXPLANATION: Part 2 of this lesson invites students to further analyze the content and meaning of free verse poetry. By trying to reconstruct a poem, they will gain understanding of the nature and structure of free verse. This will lead, we hope, to the natural next step—writing a poem of their own. Because free verse is so open-ended (no pattern or rhyme to provide form), students may discover that writing an original poem is more challenging than it looks. All this experience will pay off!

Skill Focus

Writing free verse poems

Materials & Resources

☆ Photocopies of a free verse poem for each group (see Preliminary Considerations for additional information)

Quick Hints

Remind students that the content areas they're studying can provide excellent subject matter for their poetry (as in the model poem provided in this lesson). Give students this tip for using content area material to write a poem: Select a few key topical words to build your poem around and then write the rest of the poem to represent the "big picture" idea (main concept).

Preliminary Considerations: *Using a large font and providing ample spacing between lines, type out a fairly short free verse poem on your computer. (You might choose to use one of your own favorites or the one provided in this lesson.) Make enough copies for each pair or small group. Cut out each line and place the lines into an envelope, one envelope for each pair/group.*

STEPS

1. Tell students that in this lesson they'll continue to explore free verse poetry, this time with an extra twist. They'll have a chance to try to reconstruct a poem that has been cut apart. The challenge is greater than with rhyming or patterned poetry because there are fewer clues as to how the pieces fit together.

2. Distribute an envelope to each group (see Preliminary Considerations). Direct the groups to study the lines contained in the envelope and to try to reconstruct the poem. See a sample free verse poem at right. (It's fun to include content area concepts and words, if possible; this poem incorporates science content.)

> **On the Beach**
>
> I relax on the beach
> The sun prickling my skin
> Heat radiating through my body
> I give no thought to rays
> coming from the center of the universe
> Formed of pressure and fusion
> Hydrogen colliding and smashing
> An undefined, raging mass of fire
> Infrared waves traveling light years
> through perils of the solar system
> Just to touch me on the beach
> Where I lie
> Simply, happily
> Feeling that life is good.

3. When groups have finished putting together their own versions of the poem, have each group practice reading the poem they've constructed, using their most expressive voices. Point out that the lines and punctuation should guide their pauses and expressions. Once they've practiced, invite the groups to each present a dramatic reading to the class. Try to have all students participate—either through choral reading or by having students take turns reading individually.

4. Now read the actual poem aloud twice: The first time just so that students can enjoy listening to it and the second time so groups can compare it with their own version. To conclude, invite groups to discuss which version they like best.

Writing a short response

EXPLANATION: In this lesson students learn the art of writing a short response. Not only will this help them to summarize what they've learned (which in turn helps them to process and clarify their understanding), but it will also aid them greatly in generating short responses on standardized tests.

Skill Focus

Writing short responses to discover, develop, and refine ideas; completing Exit Tickets

Materials & Resources

☆ Transparency of Exit Tickets (see Appendix, page 123)

Quick Hints

Beyond being of great benefit to students, Exit Tickets allow you to get concise, immediate feedback from lessons. This information can be an invaluable resource both for helping you analyze the effectiveness of your instruction and for planning subsequent lessons. A sample Exit Ticket is below.

EXIT TICKET

Distinguish between the terms _____ and _____:

_____
_____
_____
_____
_____

Remember that you can use Exit Tickets regularly at the closure of your lessons in all content areas, as well as in your language arts class.

STEPS

1. Tell students that this lesson focuses on how to provide a short response to a specific request for information. The short response will be written in the form of an Exit Ticket. You can use these tickets on any occasion when you feel it would be beneficial for students to summarize, compare, or define key points from a lesson and/or when you need immediate feedback. Students are required to hand you a ticket before they leave the room for another class or as they head to the cafeteria. Display a transparency of an Exit Ticket. (See Quick Hints for an example. Also see Appendix, page 123, for several blank Exit Ticket templates.)

2. Remind students that whenever they are asked to provide a short response (whether it be for Exit Tickets or any other purpose), they should follow the same process. Write the following steps on a display chart:

   • Identify the key words.
   • Identify any words or phrases on the response form that tell you what to do: for _example, identify, explain, distinguish between, give an example, give your opinion,_ etc.
   • Keep the response short and focused.

3. Model for students how to go about the process of responding. For the sample in this lesson, the Exit Ticket task is "Distinguish between the terms _conductor_ and _insulator._" First, help students focus on the key words.

4. Walk back through the text you've chosen to respond to and demonstrate how you highlight the key words _conductor_ and _insulator._

5. Model how you determine exactly what you're being asked to do. Highlight "Distinguish between"; remark that "When you _distinguish_ between two things, you tell how those things are _different._"

6. Think aloud as you recall brief definitions of the two terms from what you've studied. For example, you might say the following: "I know that a conductor is a material that allows thermal energy to flow through it easily. I also know that an insulator is a material that opposes the flow of thermal energy so that it doesn't flow through it. So I think I can summarize that important difference in one sentence." Describe, too, how you could go back to the section with those key words (either finding the page from memory or using the index) to review it before writing your summary.

7. Finally, write in the space provided on the Exit Ticket:

   A conductor is a material that allows thermal energy to flow easily through it, but an insulator blocks the flow of thermal energy.

Using the Internet to communicate

EXPLANATION: E-mail has become a popular mode of communication for all of us today. In this lesson, you can share with students your enthusiasm for using this form of communication as you review with them important rules and fun tips related to e-mail writing. This lesson also helps students identify the differences between e-mail messages and friendly letters.

Skill Focus

Using the Internet to communicate with family and friends

Materials & Resources

☆ Computer connected to the Internet, if possible

Quick Hints

As a follow-up activity, have students discuss and list the differences between e-mails and friendly letters. The following features are unique to e-mails: no date or return address (they're built into the e-mail system); "Dear—" greeting optional; emoticons or insertable graphics may be used; informal tone; no formal closing required (such as "Yours" or "Sincerely").

STEPS

1. Tell students that you realize that most of them already have experience sending and receiving e-mails. Nonetheless, everyone can benefit from a review of e-mail rules and etiquette. So that is what you will focus on today, in addition to identifying acceptable differences between e-mails and friendly letters.

2. Have students (in groups or pairs) jot down as many rules and tips about e-mail use as possible. Bring the class together and invite a spokesperson for each group to tell the class what they came up with. On a transparency or chart paper, list the guidelines. You might want to display this for ongoing reference. Below is a sample list.

Guidelines and Tips for Using E-mails

* Never say anything in an e-mail that you wouldn't want others to know about. Nothing—absolutely nothing—is truly confidential in an e-mail.

* Be careful that the tone of your e-mail can't be misinterpreted.

* Spell-check your e-mails even when you're writing to a good friend. Take advantage of this feature—it will allow you to fix careless errors.

* Don't share a friend's e-mail with others without your friend's knowledge and permission.

* You don't have to write using the format of a regular letter unless you choose to.

* In general, it's best to keep e-mails short and save long, involved letters for regular mail.

* Have fun with e-mails. Use emoticons—these neat special effects add voice to your writing.

---

3. Now model for students writing an original e-mail and sending it to a friend (get prior permission from your friend). Composing your e-mail on the computer as students watch would be most effective; however, if you don't have this technology available in your classroom, you might compose it on a transparency. Have students pay specific attention to the distinctions between this kind of message and a friendly letter (see page 84). A sample e-mail follows.

Marian, I know you enjoy keeping up with lots of great book titles to use in your classroom. I've just finished <u>The Tale of Despereaux</u> by Kate DiCamillo and want to recommend it. DiCamillo won the Newbery Award for this story, so you know it's a good one! I read it because I loved her other book, <u>Because of Winn Dixie.</u> This writer really touches the heart. I hope you'll read the new book and love it just as I did! ;-)=) Let me know. Please send me some of your book recommendations.—Cheryl

Writing for a production

Preliminary Considerations: *For a week or two before this lesson, make available to students poetry books (see Materials & Resources) that have been written for two voices. You might want to create a special display of these books in your classroom library and set up dedicated time for students to read through the books, in pairs or in small groups.*

STEPS

1. Inform students that in this lesson they'll get to do something quite different—first they'll recite a two-voice poem and then they'll write their own two-voice poems. Hold a brief discussion of this kind of literature, which should now be familiar to the class. Review these guidelines with students:

   ### In a two-voice poem

   - the position of the lines alerts the speakers to which person is doing the speaking.
   - there are two columns, one to be read aloud by each speaker.
   - the position of the line tells each speaker when to deliver his or her line.
   - occasionally, both columns have words on the same line, calling for both voices at the same time.

2. Model how to write a poem with two voices. Tell students that you want them to pay special attention, not only because they'll soon be writing a similar poem themselves but also because you'll be expecting them to perform this model poem. To add an extra element of interest, you might want to connect your poem to content the class is currently studying. The sample poem at the end of this lesson is based on an intermediate-grade unit of study on the Jurassic period. As you write, think aloud about which lines would sound best with one voice and which need the emphasis of two voices.

3. Divide the class into two groups; assign each group to be the voice of one column. After each group practices its lines, have the two groups read the poem aloud collectively several times.

4. Invite the class to evaluate the poem. Pose questions like the following to initiate the discussion:
   - Are appropriate lines emphasized with strong voices?
   - Are words split up in a logical way?
   - Are there better word choices?
   - Where do you recommend that voices become soft or loud?
   - In what ways is it clear that this type of poetry is meant to be heard rather than merely read?

EXPLANATION: One of the best reasons to have students produce a play is to give them experience facing an audience—great practice for the future. While this lesson doesn't tackle a whole play, it helps students build confidence through oral presentation. At the same time, it provides a unique writing assignment.

Skill Focus

Writing plays, scripts, productions

Materials & Resources

☆ Poetry collections of poems for two voices, such as *Joyful Noise: Poems for Two Voices* and *I Am Phoenix: Poems for Two Voices*, both by Paul Fleischman; or *Math Talk: Mathematical Ideas in Poems for Two Voices* by Theoni Pappas.

☆ A *lined* transparency

Quick Hints

When you teach writing plays, be sure to discuss the following elements of playwriting: dialogue, character development, stage directions, theme/main idea, and plot. In particular, understanding the stage directions (italicized within parentheses) and the dialogue format (spoken words after character's name, without quotation marks) helps students differentiate this kind of writing from other forms.

5. Give students an opportunity to write and produce their own poems for two voices. You might organize the class into pairs or small groups; either way, make sure that you provide time for all students to hear their works performed orally. Good topics for poems for two voices can range from geometric shapes to photosynthesis to colonialism to Shakespeare. These poems can be used to clarify and illustrate students' understanding of the content and concepts they're studying. Most of all, they're fun to compose and produce.

The Jurassic Period

It started with a crash	
	And a boom
Some worldwide disaster	Some worldwide disaster
That left many reptiles extinct	
	Plant life changed
Conifers	
	Cycads
The modern-day ginkgo	
All thrived during this time	All thrived during this time
	Skies were filled
With flying reptiles	
	The first birds evolving from dinosaurs
ZOOOOOM!	ZOOOOOM!
THUD...	THUD...
The Apatosaurus appears	
	A giant herbivore, a.k.a. Brontosaurus
Followed by others	Followed by many
Then time passed	
	Many millions of years
Listen	
	What do you hear?
The dinosaurs are no more	The dinosaurs are no more
Replaced by	
	cars,
trains,	
	planes
People rushing everywhere	
	cell phones,
computers	
Hush!	Hush!
Will it end again...	
	with a crash?

Polishing and Publishing Our Writing

It's true that students will write to please themselves. They'll write to please us as well—to achieve the grades they desire. But they'll really give it their all when they know they're writing for an audience. Once students understand that they'll be publishing for others—especially for their peers in the classroom and the school—a healthy pride kicks in. As your student writers mature and gain confidence in their writing, you'll discover that they actually want to revise and edit!

Of course, only once in a while does a piece of writing emerge that deserves real revising and editing. The writer usually recognizes right away that it's one of his or her best efforts. The revising will focus on improving word choice, organization, development, flow, and other similar elements. The editing will address conventions so that the final version includes correct spelling, punctuation, and grammar and so that the piece is typed or handwritten neatly. Not until the revising and the editing are complete will the writer have created a work that he or she can feel proud about sharing with others.

How does this process work within the classroom? As teachers, we use the Writing Workshop to model and experiment with many different types of writing for our students. Of all these drafts, we select only a few good pieces to polish through revising and editing and then publish. There are at least several good reasons for this approach.

First, we want our students to realize that not everything they write—and certainly not everything a teacher writes—is worthy of publishing. Learning to evaluate and critique one's own work is a valuable skill. By modeling our own selection process, we help students begin to develop an internal set of criteria for discerning which of their pieces are not that good, which are okay, which are pretty good, and which are outstanding.

Second, students would be overwhelmed if we tried to publish everything they wrote—the writing, revising, and editing process is simply too laborious. Having students select a few outstanding pieces of writing to polish for publication can help them to view the process as exciting rather than daunting.

The same rationale applies to the overall classroom as well. Publishing only a few pieces per student makes it a more manageable undertaking for the whole class. You'd quickly be pulling out your hair if everything students wrote had to be revised and edited extensively and then published. Having all students working on writing their rough drafts daily until they've produced perhaps three to five good pieces keeps the pace reasonable for everyone. And once all students have completed the three to five good pieces, you can hold individual conferences with them to determine which one is the very best. This will be the one that goes through the full process of revising and editing so that it can be published.

Exactly how do you publish your students' work? The broad definition is taking a piece of writing through all the phases of the writing process so that ultimately it is a clean and final, revised and edited product that is ready to be seen by others. Creating a book is a popular choice. On the informal end of the spectrum, some teachers have their students simply fold and staple pages to form booklets. Others put a little more work into the books, using computers to add fancy graphics and the like. Still others hire bookbinders to make the final product look very professional.

Beyond books, there are numerous ways to publish student work for others to see. Below are three of these possibilities.

1. You can have students write, revise, and edit personal letters that are actually mailed and delivered to the addressee.

2. You can display their work in classrooms or school hallways. For instance, you may create a permanent bulletin board on which students have assigned spaces to display their compositions for teachers, the principal, other students, parents, and staff members. This bulletin board should include a comment sheet for readers to write their own positive responses to the work.

3. You can have students create newsletters that can be sent home or delivered to other classes.

In short, it doesn't really matter what form the publication takes as long as others get to read your students' work. The idea of an audience is a tremendous motivator and reward for student writers.

This middle school's newsletter offers students the exciting experience of seeing their work in print as well as the opportunity to engage in real-life tasks of researching articles, conducting interviews, writing news features, and laying out and designing pages.

Tip for Revising and Editing

Here's a trick that we learned from a fifth-grade teacher. When students are working with a piece of writing that they plan to publish, read through it quickly before you meet with the student for a conference. Using a colored pen, place a dot in the margin for every error that the student should have caught with the Quick Check list. Read until you have ten dots in the margin. If you get to the end of the composition before reaching ten, you're ready to begin your conference. If not, stop reading and tell the student, "You're not quite ready for the conference yet. You need to go back and use the Quick Check list. Get a friend to help, if necessary. Let me know when you're ready." When the student returns with his or her paper, repeat this procedure, again stopping if you find ten errors before reaching the end. This might sound a bit harsh, but it gets results. More important, it gives students the right message—that they're in charge of applying the basics.

Using technology for revising and editing

EXPLANATION: Nothing seems to motivate students to revise and edit more than the use of a computer! Once they become comfortable with the technology (usually not at all a challenge for their generation), they quickly grasp the efficiency and flexibility that the computer provides for both revising and editing a composition. This lesson provides instruction and reinforcement in essential word-processing skills.

Skill Focus

Using basic computer skills for writing, revising, and editing

Materials & Resources

☆ Computer with word-processing capabilities

☆ Multi-paragraph piece with deliberate errors, typed and saved on your computer

☆ Photocopies (one for each student) of the Situation/Solution chart (see page 102)

☆ Revision Checklist; Final Editing Checklist (see Appendix, page 124)

Quick Hints

For additional practice, create index cards describing hypothetical situations similar to those in the left-hand column of the chart on page 102. Have students choose a card and try to find an efficient solution.

STEPS

Note: *This lesson is best taught in small groups; you might have other students engage in other Writing Workshop activities (for example, continuing to write the rough draft of a piece they're working on) while you teach each individual group at the computer. Alternatively, you might teach this lesson to the whole class in a school computer lab.*

1. Review with students the two different phases of refining/polishing a piece of writing—revising and editing. Remind them that revising is a deep, thoughtful process pertaining to idea development. Editing means cleaning up the mechanics of a piece. Both are necessary for polishing any draft that will be published and read by others. On a transparency or display chart, post the Revision Checklist and Final Editing Checklist (see Appendix, page 124). Explain that there may be some overlap between the two phases; thus, while this lesson focuses on editing, there are also references to revising.

2. Display your prepared document. Explain to students how a computer can make their editing work so much quicker and easier than it would be if they were working by hand. Today you'll model for them the most common techniques for making these changes to a draft of writing.

3. Distribute photocopies of the Situation/Solution chart (see page 102). Present each hypothetical situation to students, demonstrating how to make the proper change on the computer. Refer to the information on the chart as necessary. (Note: The directions in the "How to Accomplish" column apply to PCs. If you are using a Mac system, you will need to modify appropriately. In any case, we advise checking all the directions in that column with the computer you are actually using in your classroom before presenting them to the class; there may be minor variations, even among PCs.)

4. After demonstrating each solution for students, close the document without saving the changes you made to the original. Have volunteers choose a situation and sit at the computer to implement the required change.

SITUATION	SOLUTION	HOW TO ACCOMPLISH
You've discovered that a few lines of the text don't seem to be in the logical place.	Move the lines without having to retype them.	Place cursor in front of beginning letter of the passage being moved. Left-click on the mouse and, keeping the button down, move the mouse to highlight all words that need to be repositioned. Release the mouse button, leaving text highlighted. (This is called selecting text.) Click on the scissors icon on the toolbar, which should "cut out" the desired text. Place the cursor at the location where you want to position the text. Click on the clipboard icon to "paste" it in.
You've capitalized all the letters of your title, but you think it would look better with only the first letter of each word in capitals.	Make this change without retyping.	Highlight the text as directed above. Left-click on Format on the menu bar. Scroll to Change Case and choose Title Case.
You want to check the spelling.	Make as many changes as possible without retyping or consulting a dictionary.	Review the document and search for words that have a red underlining. Place the cursor on the word and right-click. If the correct spelling appears, place the cursor on the correct word and click. (Note: On most PC programs, misspelled words are automatically underlined. If not, be sure to activate the feature by left-clicking on Tools and then left-clicking on Spelling and Grammar.)
You want to spot check for grammatical errors.	Make as many changes as possible without retyping.	Review the document and search for all text that has been underlined in green. Right-click on the text and consider what the grammar check says. Make the change only if necessary; often you'll find that no change is needed.
You want your teacher or a peer to review a section of text that you're not sure makes sense. You want to point out this section to him or her.	Highlight the text in a color so the reader can easily identify the section you want him or her to consider.	On the formatting toolbar, left-click on Highlight or left-click on the Highlight icon on your toolbar (an "abc" and a pen). Select the text you want to highlight. You can choose the color you wish to use.
You need to find a reference you made to a certain item in your text quickly.	Look at each reference without reading back over the whole text.	Click on Edit on the menu bar. Scroll down to Find. In the window that appears, type in the exact word you're searching for. It will show you all of the references to that word in your document.
You want to consider changing a sentence, but you want to compare it with your new version before you replace it.	Strike through the old sentence and add the new sentence.	Select the text you want to consider eliminating. Click on Format on the menu bar and click on Fonts. A window will open. Under the section on Effects, click in the box that says Strikethrough. A line will appear in your highlighted text. Now place the cursor where you want to add your new text and type it in.

Using resources for spelling

Preliminary Considerations: *In preparation for this lesson, examine samples of students' writing. Select and record frequently misspelled words, making sure to find examples of irregular words, compound words, homophones, and common word patterns.*

EXPLANATION: The well-read student develops a sense of the way words should be spelled because he or she has seen them many times (Atwell, 1987). Yet there are many students who freeze in their writing when they do not know how to spell a word. This lesson focuses on helping students use appropriate resources for spelling.

Skill Focus

Using classroom resources for spelling; using correct spelling for frequently used words and common word patterns

Materials & Resources

☆ Word Walls; age-appropriate dictionaries and thesauruses; computer spell-checker

☆ Student writing samples from which you've culled common incorrect spellings

Quick Hints

Create an index card file of interesting ways to remember unusual spellings. For example:

● *Succeed*—"It takes double letters to succeed."

● *Wednesday*—"We hope to wed on Wednesday."

Invite students to create their own mnemonic devices to remember hard-to-spell words and to record these for other students' use. (Check first that the spelling is correct and that the mnemonic really works!)

STEPS

1. Remind students that when we want to craft a rough draft into a polished piece and share it with other people, we must work hard to get it just right. This includes making sure words are spelled correctly. Explain that in this lesson you will present a composition with quite a few spelling errors. Inform students that these are real errors that you have gathered over time from their own writing.

2. Model writing a paragraph that includes the words you have culled from student writing. As you misspell the words, think aloud about the confusing part of each word. With students' help, read back through the piece and circle the misspelled words. A sample paragraph follows.

A new vacum cleaner has just been released. The pamlet describes how well it cleans, why it is safe for the invironment, and its hith and width. If your looking for a new cleaning machine, than you'll love this vacum cleaner accept for the price! We won't withold this news from you. It is only $1,000!

(*Answer key: vacuum; pamphlet; environment; height; you're; then; vacuum; except; withhold*)

3. Now model how you check for the correct spelling of the words. Demonstrate how you refer to classroom Word Walls as well as to the dictionary and thesaurus. If possible, type the paragraph into a computer document to demonstrate the use of the spell-checker. (Note: Point out to students that the spell-checker will correct many misspelled words automatically—it will change *vacum* to *vacuum*, for instance; however, it will not indicate the incorrect homophone spelling—*you're* for *your* or *then* for *than.* While the grammar checker will alert students to these kinds of errors, they will probably need to consult a dictionary or thesaurus to confirm the correct word.)

Revising and editing with a checklist

EXPLANATION: Applying criteria from simple checklists helps students focus on critical writing components. The checklist in this lesson is designed to work with the earlier lesson on writing a friendly letter (see page 84). Encouraging students to use this checklist provides an extra benefit—they are required to work with partners and to give and accept constructive peer criticism.

Skill Focus

Using a simple checklist for revising and editing; working independently and collaboratively

Materials & Resources

☆ Students' original friendly letters (from lesson on page 84, or from other class work)

☆ Photocopies (one for each student) of Checklist for a Friendly Letter (see Step 3)

☆ Revision Checklist and Final Editing Checklist (see Appendix, page 124)

Quick Hints

Invite students to keep this checklist (and others like it) as a resource. To organize these kinds of resources, students can three-hole punch the pages for storage in a writing binder, paste them into a student-generated writing handbook, or tuck them away in a pocket folder.

STEPS

1. Review with students the Revision Checklist and the Final Editing Checklist (introduced on page 101 and reproduced in the Appendix, page 124). Discuss how these checklists can be used to evaluate any piece of writing that students are taking beyond the rough draft stage.

2. Tell the class that instead of using these general forms, it is sometimes helpful to evaluate a specific piece of writing with a checklist tailored to that genre. In this lesson students will have a chance to check their friendly letters (see page 84) against criteria designed just for this kind of writing. And after they check their own work, they will also elicit feedback from a classmate.

3. Instruct students to get out their letters, which should be stored in their writing folders. Allow them time to review and identify the salient parts of the letter. Then distribute photocopies of the Checklist for a Friendly Letter (see below). Have each student use the checklist to evaluate his or her letter.

CHECKLIST FOR A FRIENDLY LETTER		
Self	Peer	
		I have included the date, salutation, body, and closing for a friendly letter.
		My writing sounds like me.
		The letter includes interesting news.
		I have included questions to the reader.
		My writing is legible and free of grammar, punctuation, and spelling errors.
		I have read over my letter to check for inclusion of the specific information that I needed/wished to include.
Peer Comment:		

4. After this self-evaluation, direct students to exchange their letters with a partner. Partners are to read each other's letters, fill out the checklist (using the "Peer" column), and write several helpful comments in the space provided. Peers should strive to include three positive observations and one comment about an aspect of the letter they believe could be improved. (Many teachers call this "three pluses and a wish.") Allow students time to reread their letters as they reflect on their partner's comments.

Using organizational features with informational writing

EXPLANATION: As students tackle informational text, they often ignore features built in by authors and publishers to aid comprehension. This lesson explains how those features work and encourages students to experiment with them in their own writing.

Skill Focus

Using organizational features of printed text such as page numbers and chapter headings

Materials & Resources

☆ Model page (first page of a textbook chapter) from a content textbook that includes organizational features

☆ Transparency of a schematic drawing of this page (see Preliminary Considerations)

☆ Photocopies (one for each student) of the schematic drawing

Quick Hints

For additional informational book features, hold "book feature drills." Divide the class into teams and call out questions. The first team to find the designated feature gets a point. For example, call out, "What feature could I use to find out all the pages that discuss Hiawatha in this book?" (*The index*) or "Where could I find the definition of *hogan*?" (*The glossary*)

Preliminary Considerations: *In preparation for this lesson, use the model content textbook page as the basis for a schematic drawing. (If you're not an artist, just try your best—all that's needed here is a relatively simple representation!) For each text feature on the page, sketch in a proportionately sized geometric shape that corresponds to that feature. For example, at right is a page from a social studies book.*

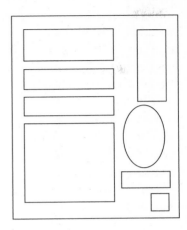

STEPS

1. Tell students that this lesson focuses on key organizational features that are built into almost all content area texts. These features are included for one primary reason: to help readers better interpret and understand the information. With students, brainstorm and list the most common informational text features. Guide students, as needed, to include the following:

Visuals/graphics	Text	Captions	Page Numbers
Headings	Index	Subheadings	Glossary
Table of Contents		Marginal Notes	

2. Distribute copies of the schematic drawing to students (individuals, partners, or small groups). Instruct them to use their knowledge of text organization and the list you've brainstormed to try to fill in the geometric shapes with the features they represent. Give students about five minutes to discuss and label their drawings. (Note that we provide an answer key below. However, some answers may vary. For example, valid arguments could be made that the second and third blocks in the left column are headings, subheadings, or text. Remember that students' awareness and understanding are most important.)

3. Bring the class together. Invite volunteers to come forward to label the various shapes on the transparency. Ask students to explain their decisions and to describe how they use that feature in text as they read.

4. Challenge students to use some of these features in their own informational writing so that their readers will benefit.

Answers: Left column, top to bottom: Heading; subheading; subheading; text. Right column, top to bottom: Marginal notes; visuals/graphics; caption; page number.

Listening to and responding to others' writing

EXPLANATION: Reading aloud to an audience is key to reinforcing the concept that writing is communication (Tully, 1996). Just as we encourage students to read with partners, it's valuable to have them work in pairs to respond to each other's writing. Peer conferencing offers a context for this. This lesson provides a safe structure—a student-generated response form—to encourage students to respond to each other's writing.

Skill Focus

Listening carefully and responding in constructive ways to others' writing

Materials & Resources

☆ Transparency of Peer Response to Writing Form (see Appendix, page 125)

☆ Photocopies (one for each student) of this form

☆ Rough drafts of writing, selected from students' folders

Quick Hints

In order to facilitate ongoing, regular peer conferencing, dedicate a particular area of the classroom to be the "conference corner." Store response forms, clipboards, tape recorders, a timer, and so on in this area. Establish rules and procedures

STEPS

1. Review with students how helpful it is for writers to receive feedback from their readers. Without such feedback it is much harder for the writer to judge whether a piece is successful or not because, after all, a primary goal of writing is to communicate. Help students understand how in a creative writing workshop (for instance, in college or at a writing institute), each person gets a chance to read a rough draft of a piece of writing out loud to a group. Then the group evaluates that piece. Good listening habits, as well as the ability to give and take constructive criticism, are essential. Explain that in this lesson students will have the chance to read a first or second draft aloud. They'll read to one peer at a time and use a form to help structure the feedback.

2. Display your transparency of the Peer Response to Writing Form. Note that this form is deliberately incomplete. In addition to the Summary section, seven lines have been left blank. Students can fill in these lines with self-generated and/or class-generated questions.

3. Now brainstorm with the class appropriate open-ended questions to ask about a piece of writing. Remind them that if the questions are thoughtful and well constructed, the writer will be more likely to do a good job of evaluating his or her writing. A list of possible questions follows.

   * Who is your audience for this piece?
   * What part of your piece do you think works best?
   * What part of your piece does not work for you?
   * What will you do next with this piece of writing?
   * Do you need help?

   Model on the transparency how you write in these questions on your form. Point out that in addition to asking well-targeted questions, partners can help each other by discussing and summarizing a writing plan. Call attention to that part of the form.

4. Distribute a photocopy of the Response Form to each student. Instruct students to follow your transparency model and write in questions (either their own or the questions brainstormed by the class). See page 107 for one possible completed form.

5. Finally, have students select a piece of their original writing that is still in the first- or second-draft stage. Organize the class into pairs and have each student in the pair listen to the other's piece and use the form to provide feedback. If you wish students to elicit feedback from more than one peer, photocopy and distribute additional forms and form new partner groups.

ahead of time—such as limits to the number of pairs who may conference at one time—and encourage students to use some of their independent writing time to set up their own conferences.

PEER RESPONSE TO WRITING FORM	Yes	No
I listened respectfully while the writing was being read aloud.		
I asked appropriate questions such as:		
Who is your audience for this piece?		
What part works best for you?		
What part does not work for you?		
What will you do next with this piece of writing?		
Do you need help?		
We summarized reflections and actions to be taken.		
Summary		

Analyzing and sharing one's writing

EXPLANATION: Just as talking about books with friends motivates readers and builds their confidence, talking about one's writing with others can provide a different and broader perspective of the composing process. This lesson has two prongs, offering students a fun technique for first examining and analyzing their own writing and then discussing it with their peers.

Skill Focus

Analyzing one's own writing; sharing writing orally with others

Materials & Resources

☆ Precut 3" x 3" sticky-notes (one for each student) as described here: Cut a large sticky-note four times, forming five horizontal strips, each sufficient for a student to write on. (Cut into the note toward the sticky part, leaving the strips attached so that they resemble fingers.)

☆ Rough draft of your writing

Quick Hints

Use the Sticky Points technique in a variety of ways. For example: (1) students can take turns sharing their points in a small group. Each student shares one point until everyone has had a turn, then each continues to his/her second point, and so forth; (2) students can use this method to structure their sharing of a piece of writing with the whole class.

STEPS

1. Explain to students that it's helpful for all writers—students as well as published authors—to be able to take a step back and survey their own writing. Writers need to be able to ask themselves what works and what doesn't. In this lesson you'll model a sharing technique for them called Sticky Points. Not only is this technique helpful for refining and improving their own writing; it allows them to share their writing with others and to help their classmates grow as writers.

2. Discuss with the class and list on a transparency things that students might want to think about while considering a piece of writing. Point out that these items don't have to be earth-shattering, just aspects they'd like to focus on and become more aware of. A sample list follows.

   - Something I need help with
   - A very precise word choice
   - Words that reflect voice
   - My favorite part
   - A problem I encountered
   - Character development
   - A technique I've tried

   - An interesting word
   - A figure of speech
   - Sensory words
   - Transitions
   - The story climax
   - Main idea
   - An important event/idea

3. Display a transparency of a preselected rough draft of your own writing. As you read through the piece, think aloud about elements from the list that strike you as needing attention. For each item you identify, tear off a "finger" of the sticky-note and attach it to the text at that spot. Mark places until you've used all the fingers on your sticky-note.

4. Tell students that you're now prepared to discuss your work with a partner. Invite a volunteer to come forward. He or she should use the points on your sticky-note fingers to initiate a discussion with you about your piece.

5. Encourage students to practice this sharing technique. Following your model, they should choose a composition from their folders, study it for strengths and weaknesses, and place the four sticky-note fingers on items they've identified. Then they should turn to a partner and use those points to initiate a discussion.

Reflecting about writing and setting goals to guide future writing

EXPLANATION: As Nancie Atwell observes in her classic *In the Middle* (1987), writers often overlook their most important readers—themselves—and instead depend on others to identify and solve problems in their writing. This lesson builds on the previous one, providing students with another concrete tool to use in setting goals.

Skill Focus

Reviewing own writing to set goals for growth

Materials & Resources

☆ Transparency and photocopies (several for each student) of Writing Reflection Form (see Appendix, page 126)

☆ Rough draft of a brief piece of your writing

Quick Hints

You may want to (at least partially) evaluate students' writing progress by assessing how well they have achieved their individual goals. The following scale could be used.

- **Excellent:** Completely accomplished all 3 goals
- **Satisfactory:** Accomplished 2 of 3 goals
- **Fair:** Accomplished 1 of 3 goals
- **Unsatisfactory:** Accomplished 0 of 3 goals

STEPS

Note: *Although we have not broken this lesson into parts, it works best if taught over a period of days. Students may need to focus on one question at a time to develop genuine understanding.*

1. Remind students of the Sticky Points technique they already know for analyzing their writing. Tell them that this lesson provides another means of examining their own writing for ways that it might be improved. They will learn to use a special form with questions that will help them to focus on specific strengths and weaknesses in a piece of their own writing.

2. Copy onto the chalkboard a preselected piece of your writing. Using a transparency, display the Writing Reflection Form (see Appendix, page 126). Read your piece to the class, then think aloud about each question on the form as you evaluate your draft. Demonstrate how you fill in the form with your answers, including the process you use to define goals for your future writing. A sample passage and filled-in form are below.

The Glacier

Were my eyes playing tricks on me? When we were closer to the glacier, I began to see a vibrant blue color spread through the ice. Why did I expect the glacier to resemble white packed snow? The billions of ice crystals shown in the bright morning sun.

WRITING REFLECTION FORM

Writing Mode: Circle Choice Narrative Expository Persuasive (Descriptive)
Writing Form: Circle Choice Story Letter Poem Play (Essay)
Other: _____

What is the skill focus of this writing?	When I wrote this piece we were writing to use adjectives to describe.
What did I learn from this writing?	I learned that writing description can be fun and that I have to close my eyes and imagine the topic.
What part of the writing am I most proud of?	I really like the way I started my writing with a question.
What would I do differently if I had this writing to do over again?	If I did this writing again, I believe I would work on making the verbs stronger. For example, I would use the verb "inched" in place of "were" in the second sentence.

GOALS FOR GROWTH

1. One of my goals will be to use my thesaurus more to find stronger verbs.

2. I also think I will work on using all of the five senses in my descriptions.

3. I also need to be sure to add an interesting conclusion to my writing.

3. Distribute several copies of this form to each student for ongoing use.

Publishing writing

EXPLANATION: For perhaps that most basic of reasons—most writers write to be read—publishing is an important stage in the writing process (Atwell, 1987). This multiday lesson takes students through all the steps, beginning with their selecting a topic of interest—a career in a particular content field (see Note)—and ending with their binding a book to share with others.

Skill Focus

Researching and writing personal narratives, interview questions, and multi-paragraph reports; publishing in various formats

Materials & Resources

☆ Textbooks, trade books, online resources (see Quick Hints list), and other sources of career information

☆ Sample facts about a career in a content-related field (from sources such as those listed above)

☆ 3 sample entries for your modeled booklet

☆ File folders, notebook paper, construction paper or poster paper

☆ Staples, glue, or other bookbinding material

Quick Hints

Here's a sampling of Web sites you might recommend to students for this lesson. Some are

STEPS

Note: *Although we have not broken this lesson into parts, it should be considered a multiday lesson. The focus of the first two days is on your modeling how to select a topic and generate the three kinds of journal entries. The focus of subsequent days is on students' research, development of their own entries, and publishing of the journals.*

The basis for students' research and writing in this project is investigation and reflection about content-related careers. Focusing on careers in a particular field requires students to examine that field from both factual and personal perspectives. You can explore careers in almost any field that relates to subject matter your class is studying in science, social studies, literature, or other content areas.

1. Introduce this lesson by telling the class that several days of Writing Workshop will be devoted to publishing individual books. Tell students that they will have the opportunity to write three related but diverse pieces about a content-related career area, format these as entries in a booklet, and finally publish their journals to share with the class. The three diverse entries will comprise these three tasks:

   • **Entry #1:** Write a "personal reaction" paragraph, describing why you would be interested in a particular career.

   • **Entry #2:** Develop interview questions for a person in this career.

   • **Entry #3:** Write a multi-paragraph report about this chosen career and an opinion about the field of study.

   Explain that you will model each of these processes, based on a topic you have selected and researched. Then it will be students' turn to gather data and generate original entries.

2. On a transparency, use a chart format to present an array of possible careers. In this lesson, we focus on science careers that pertain to work with animals and/or the environment. A sample chart identifying and defining those careers, as well as listing well-known people connected to those careers, follows.

Career	Skills	Person
Animal Behaviorist	Studies how animals interact and how animals meet their basic needs	Jane Goodall
Ecologist	Studies plants and animals in their environment	Henry Chandler Cowles
Behavioral Ecologist	Researches habitats and breeding of different species Studies conservation of biological diversity	Wendy Jackson
Limnologist	Studies freshwater lakes and streams and animals in that habitat	Ruth Patrick
Explorer	Uncovers new species of animals Leads expeditions to unusual and uncommon habitats	Richard Wiese
Fish Hatchery Manager	Studies fish habitats and supplies fish for local rivers, lakes, etc.	Robert Stickney

Note: Other related careers include zoologist, veterinarian, lab technician, field researcher, zoo educator, conservationist.

general in nature; others address specific careers.

www.askjeeves.com

www.fmnh.org/exhibits/exhibit_ sites/wis/activities

www.cnr.colostate.edu/careers/ fisherybiocareeroverview

www.sandiegozoo.org/kids/job_ profiles

www.enchantedlearning.com

www.scilinks.org

To provide students with valuable experience in interviewing, invite a guest, who is well known in the community (TV meteorologist, high school principal, mayor, etc.), to visit the class. Guide students in conducting an interview with the guest. Use sample questions from Step 5 of this lesson to conduct the interview. Direct students to compile the information from the interview to write a brief informational paragraph about the guest.

3. Model how you think aloud to choose the career of fish hatchery manager. For example, you might say, "My most pleasant memories are from the times I have spent around ponds and lakes! I'm thinking this career would give me the opportunity to have fun and help the environment, too." Next, using a transparency, model writing the first entry. Remind students that first-person narrative writing includes first-person pronouns (*I, we, me, my*) and interesting details. A sample personal reaction paragraph follows.

> If I were to choose a career in the environmental field, it would have to relate to rivers, lakes, and streams. I love the water and I can't think of a better place to spend my working time. I think a fish hatchery manager career would allow me to study fish habitats and move fish from the hatchery to rivers, lakes, or streams. I could spend many happy hours outdoors with fish and fishermen.

4. Review the writing by asking the students to check for basic conventions and other criteria, such as the following:
   - Identifying first-person pronouns
   - Finding interesting details
   - Identifying various types of sentence structure (simple, compound, complex with prepositional phrases).

5. Follow the same process for the second entry—the interview questions. Demonstrate for students how you generate good interview questions targeted to the career you have selected. As you model writing these questions, review these criteria for students:
   - To form your questions, think of specific information you would like to know.
   - Design questions that target this kind of information and that help you focus your thinking.
   - Generate questions that require more than *yes* or *no* answers.

   Here are some sample questions that fit the above criteria:
   - What made you want to be a _____?
   - Who influenced your work?

- Where did you learn the most helpful information about your field?
- How does your work impact the future?

Note that if it's feasible and practical, you might work with students to set up actual interviews of a person in a selected field. Otherwise, or in addition, students might use their questions to help organize the research they do for the next entry of this project. Thus, as they read about their chosen field, they might use this interview question format to help them gather information. For example, if they were researching "Animal Behaviorists," they might use a question like "Who influenced your work?" to help them focus on and assemble facts about early animal behaviorists and how their work affected the field.

6. Next, model how you plan and compose your third entry—the multi-paragraph report and your concluding opinion statement. For example, you might say:

> I remember that I must present the overall idea about my chosen career of fish hatchery manager in my first paragraph. Next, I need to explain at least three characteristics of this field of study. Each characteristic with supporting details will become a separate paragraph. My concluding paragraph will revisit my overall idea expressed in the first paragraph, but this time I'll include my opinion about the career.

You might also refer to the lesson on page 32 for criteria and further information about writing multiple paragraph informational essays. The Quick Hints section on page 87 lists criteria, as well.

7. Once you have modeled all three entries, have students select a career from the chart and begin their own research, using the resources you've made available or referred them to. Employing tools they should be familiar with by now (see page 25), they can take notes in a number of ways—for example, on a graphic organizer or on note cards. See, too, the suggestions about gathering research in Step 5. (You may need to remind students to write their notes in words and phrases, not complete sentences.)

8. For the next several days, have students work on their entries. As students research and write, circulate around the room, checking to make sure they are following your modeling. Because these entries are to be published, students need to polish their work. Remind them to use the Revision and Final Editing Checklists (see Appendix, page 124) as they take their pieces from rough to final draft.

9. When the booklets are complete, invite students to staple or otherwise bind the pages (for instance, they might hole-punch the left-hand margin and tie it with yarn). Now the booklets are ready to be displayed proudly in the classroom—perhaps shelved in the classroom library or fastened to a bulletin board.

Name: _____ Date: _____

A STORY MAP

Selection: _____

SETTING	
Place:	
Time:	
CHARACTERS	
PLOT/EVENTS	
Beginning:	
Middle:	
End:	

CAMERA GRAPHIC ORGANIZER

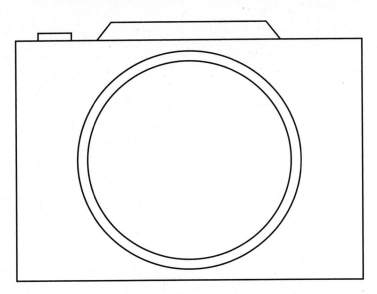

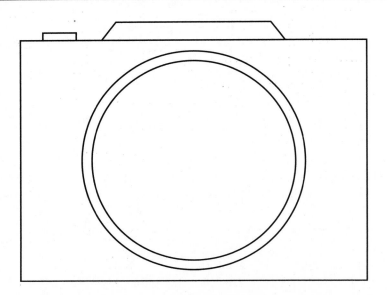

USES OF CONJUNCTIONS

TYPE	CONJUNCTION
Coordinating	and, but, for, or, nor, so, yet
Correlative	either . . . or
Subordinating	neither . . . nor
	not only . . . but also
	both . . . and
	whether . . . or
	just as . . . so
	after, although, as, as if, as long as, as though, because, before, if, in order that, provided that, rather than, since, though, till, unless, until, when, where, whereas, while

USES OF COLONS

USE	EXAMPLE
Salutation of a business letter	Dear Sirs: Dear Governor Edwards:
To separate hours and minutes in written time	6:32 p.m.
To introduce a list	The following students are attending: John, Jessica, Martha, Emory, and Tyesha.
To emphasize a word, phrase, or clause	There was only one excuse: ignorance!
To separate title and subtitle, volume and page, and chapter and verse in literature	*World War II: The Greatest War*, World Book B:311, John 3:16
To introduce a sentence, question, or quotation (formal use)	Faramir, in *Lord of the Rings*, said these words: "I do not believe this darkness will endure."

RULES FOR CAPITALIZATION

USE	EXAMPLE
Direct quotes	"Let's get started!" shouted the coach. "I'm thinking," he said, "that it's time to start." He shouted, "Let's get started!"
Names of people	Judy, Jim, Paul Angiolillo
Geographical names	Germany, Glacier National Park, Main Street, Mississippi River, North America, Rocky Mountains, South Carolina, the South
Holidays	Christmas, Easter, Fourth of July, Halloween, Hanukkah, Thanksgiving
Historical periods	Enlightenment, Industrial Age, Middle Ages, Pleistocene Era, Renaissance
Brand names	Doritos, Honda, Izod, Kleenex, Windex
Special events	Boston Tea Party, Civil War, Great Depression, Illinois State Fair, Mardi Gras, Super Tuesday, World War II
Organizations	Democratic National Committee, Red Cross, Salvation Army, United Way
Nationalities and races	American, French, Japanese, African American, Caucasian
Languages	English, French, German, Italian
Religions	Christianity, Hinduism, Islam, Judaism
Headlines and book titles	"Aliens Spotted Over Desert," Charlotte's Web
Works of art	*American Gothic* (Grant Wood), *The Starry Night* (Vincent Van Gogh), *Swans Reflecting as Elephants* (Salvador Dalí)
Newspapers, magazines	*New York Times, Southern Living*
Musical compositions	"Pomp and Circumstance," "The Star-Spangled Banner," "A Hard Day's Night"
First word in every sentence	We are going to the football game on Friday.
Days and months	Monday, Tuesday, Wednesday, January, June, December
Titles and abbreviations of titles	Senator Block, Rev. Dogood, Dr. Healer, President Michaels, Mrs. Plum, Mr. Raley, Judge Right

Just-Right Writing Mini-Lessons: Grades 4–6 SCHOLASTIC TEACHING RESOURCES

USE OF COMMAS

USE	EXAMPLE
To separate words, phrases, or clauses in a series of three or more items	My favorite foods are shrimp, chocolate, and asparagus. I'm going to spend my summer reading good books, swimming in the pool, and shopping at the mall.
To separate two independent clauses joined by a coordinating conjunction	The test was long and tiring, but I didn't think it was difficult.
To separate adjectives that equally modify the same noun	We took a long, tiring, difficult test.
To set off an explanatory word/phrase or an appositive that is not essential to the meaning of the sentence	This book, unlike the one I read last, is exciting! Mr. Snelgrove, the principal of our school, was at the opening of the new ball field.
To set off quoted material from the rest of the sentence	"To get to the mall," he answered, "you'll need to go six blocks and turn right." He said, "You'll need to go six blocks and turn right." "You'll need to go six blocks and turn right," he said.
To separate an adverbial clause or modifying phrase from the independent clause that follows	In the beginning of the school year, we were all excited about having homework.
To separate items in an address (Note: There is no comma between state and zip code)	You can send the box to me at 123 Main Street, Columbia, SC 29205.
To set apart person being addressed in the sentence (also called the vocative)	I told you, Jeffrey, that I would meet you after school. Tina, can you come to my house today?
To separate items in a date (Note: There is no comma between the month and the year when the day is not given)	On September 15, 2005, we went on a field trip to the Capitol. In September 2005 we went on a field trip.
To set apart words and phrases that interrupt a sentence	I was thinking, though, that we might go to the mall together.
To separate numbers in a series	1,253,672
To set off *yes* and *no* responses in a sentence	Yes, I'm going to join you at the mall.

Note: *Commas are the most frequently used punctuation mark.*
These are some of the uses appropriate for grades 4–6.

Name: _____ Date: _____

BRAINSTORMING CHART

Name of Person: _____

FEELINGS	ACTIONS	DESCRIPTION	SETTING

Just-Right Writing Mini-Lessons: Grades 4–6 SCHOLASTIC TEACHING RESOURCES

BIO-POEM FORMAT

Line 1   **Begin with first name of the character**

Line 2   **4 words to describe a relationship**

Line 3   **"Lover of" (list 3 items)**

Line 4   **"Who feels" (list 3 items)**

Line 5   **"Who fears" (list 3 items)**

Line 6   **"Who would like to" (list 3 items)**

Line 7   **"Resident of" (state setting)**

Line 8   **End with last name of the character**

- -

_____

_____ _____ _____ _____

Lover of _____, _____, _____

Who feels _____,

_____, _____,

Who fears _____,

_____, _____,

Who would like to _____,

_____, _____,

Resident of _____

_____

SUMMARIZING ORGANIZER

WHAT'S INTERESTING (Include small details in this column.)	WHAT'S IMPORTANT (Include main ideas and key details in this column.)

SUMMARY OF WHAT WAS READ

PERSUASIVE WRITING FLOW CHART

MY OPINION:

Facts and Examples for Support:

Facts and Examples for Support:

Facts and Examples for Support:

Audience:

EXPOSITORY WRITING FLOW CHART

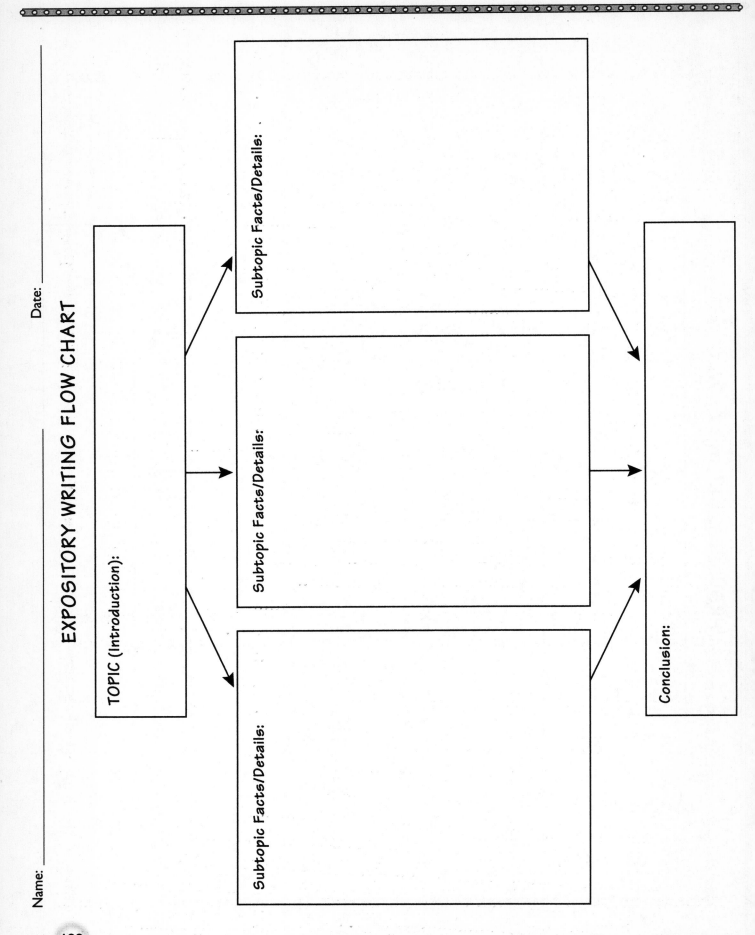

TOPIC (Introduction):

Subtopic Facts/Details:

Subtopic Facts/Details:

Subtopic Facts/Details:

Conclusion:

EXIT TICKETS

EXIT TICKET

Here's a summary of what I learned: _____

_____

_____

_____

_____

EXIT TICKET

What I learned today that will make me a better writer: _____

_____

_____

_____

_____

EXIT TICKET

How I would explain the difference between _____ and _____ :

_____

_____

_____

_____

Name: _____ Date: _____

REVISION CHECKLIST

I read my writing out loud.

To myself _____   To a friend _____   To a group _____

I asked if my writing made sense.   _____

My writing was organized with a beginning, middle, and end.   _____

My ideas were original, well developed, and appropriately sequenced. _____

I stayed focused on the topic.   _____

I used a variety of sentence types and lengths.   _____

I used interesting words that are appropriate for my audience.   _____

My writing sounded like me. (voice)   _____

Name: _____ Date: _____

FINAL EDITING CHECKLIST

I used capitals in the right places.   _____

I ended each sentence with appropriate punctuation
and used other punctuation to help my readers.   _____

I checked my grammar.   _____

I checked my spelling.   _____

My final copy is neat, legible, and appealing.   _____

Name: _____ Date: _____

PEER RESPONSE TO WRITING FORM

	YES	NO
I listened respectfully while the writing was being read aloud.		
I asked appropriate questions such as:*		
We summarized reflections and actions to be taken.		

SUMMARY

_____

_____

_____

_____

_____

_____

_____

_____

* The following lines have been left blank so that students can write in their own questions.

Name: _____ Date: _____

WRITING REFLECTION FORM

Writing Mode: Circle Choice	Narrative Expository Persuasive Descriptive
Writing Form: Circle Choice	Story Letter Poem Play Essay
	Other: _____

What is the skill focus of this writing?	_____ _____
What did I learn from this writing?	_____ _____
What part of the writing am I most proud of?	_____ _____
What would I do differently if I had this writing to do over again?	_____ _____

GOALS FOR GROWTH

1. _____

_____

2. _____

_____

3. _____

_____

Bibliography

Atwell, Nancie. *In the Middle*. Portsmouth, NH: Heinemann, 1987.

Bradby, Marie. *More Than Anything Else*. New York: Scholastic, Orchard Books, 1995.

Brown, Marc. *Arthur's Teacher Moves In*. Boston: Little, Brown, 2000.

Calkins, Lucy, and Shelley Harwayne. *Living Between the Lines*. Portsmouth, NH: Heinemann, 1991.

Creech, Sharon. *Love That Dog*. New York: HarperCollins, 2001.

Crossley-Holland, Kevin. *Arthur: The Seeing Stone*. New York: Scholastic, Arthur A. Levine Books, 2001.

Dahl, Roald. *Boy: Tales of Childhood*. New York: Puffin Books, 1986.

DiCamillo, Kate. *The Tale of Despereaux*. Cambridge, MA: Candlewick Press, 2003.

Emory, Jerry. *Dirty, Rotten, Dead?* New York: Harcourt Brace, 1996.

Fleischman, Paul. *I Am Phoenix: Poems for Two Voices*. New York: HarperTrophy, 1989.

Fleischman, Paul. *Joyful Noise: Poems for Two Voices*. New York: HarperTrophy, 1992.

Fletcher, Ralph, and Joann Portalupi. *Craft Lessons*. New York: Stenhouse, 1998.

Fletcher, Ralph. *What a Writer Needs*. Portsmouth, NH: Heinemann, 1993.

Gambrell, L.B., and P.S. Koskinen. "Imagery: A Strategy for Enhancing Comprehension." In *Comprehension Instruction: Research-Based Best Practices,* edited by C.C. Block and M. Pressley. New York: Guilford Press, 2002.

Gerstein, Mordicai. *The Man Who Walked Between the Towers*. Brookfield, CT: Roaring Brook Press, 2004.

Grimes, Nikki. *Dark Sons*. New York: Hyperion Books for Children, 2005.

Grimes, Nikki. *A Pocketful of Poems*. Boston: Houghton Mifflin Company, 2001.

Haddix, Margaret Peterson. *Among the Hidden*. New York: Aladdin, 1998.

Harcourt Science, Grade 5: How Earthquakes Are Measured. Orlando, FL: Harcourt, 2000.

Harpaz, Beth J. "Writer's Bloc: Follow the Footsteps of Famous Authors in Maine's Historic Towns," *The State Newspaper*, Associated Press, June 29, 2005.

Hillocks, G., Jr. *Research on Written Composition: New Directions for Teaching*. Urbana, IL: National Conference on Research in English/ERIC Clearinghouse on Reading and Communication Skills, 1986.

Hillocks, G., Jr., and M. W. Smith. "Grammars and Literacy Learning." In *Handbook of Research on Teaching the English Language Arts, 2nd ed.,* edited by J. Flood, D. Lapp, J. R. Squire, and J. M. Jensen. Mahwah, NJ: Erlbaum, 2003.

Hoyt, Linda. *Revisit, Reflect, Retell*. Portsmouth, NH: Heinemann, 1998.

Jacobs, A. J. *The Know-It-All*. New York: Simon & Schuster Adult Publishing Group, 2004.

Korman, Gordon. *The 6th Grade Nickname Game*. New York: Hyperion, 1998.

Lester, Julius. *John Henry*. New York: Dial, 1994.

Lewis, C.S. *Letters to Children*. New York: Scribner, 1985.

London, Jack. *To Build a Fire and Other Stories.* New York: Bantam Classics, 1986.

Lowry, Lois. *Looking Back: A Book of Memories.* New York: Houghton Mifflin, Walter Lorraine Books, 1998.

Lowry, Lois. *Number the Stars.* New York: Dell Publishing, 1989.

Masoff, Joy. *Oh, Yuck! The Encyclopedia of Everything Nasty!* New York: Workman Publishing, 2000.

Mayberry, Jodine. *Business Leaders Who Built Financial Empires.* Austin, TX: Raintree Steck-Vaughn, 1995.

Pappas, Theoni. *Math Talk: Mathematical Ideas in Poems for Two Voices.* San Carlos, CA: Wide World Publishing, 1991.

Paulsen, Gary. *Canyons.* New York: Bantam Doubleday Dell Books for Young Readers, 1990.

Paulsen, Gary. *Dogsong.* New York: Simon & Schuster, 1985.

Rylant, Cynthia. *Appalachia: The Voices of Sleeping Birds.* Orlando, FL: Harcourt Brace Jovanovich, 1991.

Sigmon, Cheryl M., and Sylvia M. Ford. *Writing Lessons for the Content Areas.* New York: Scholastic, 2005.

Silverstein, Shel. *Where the Sidewalk Ends.* New York: Harper and Row, 1974.

Steig, William. *Shrek!* New York: Farrar, Straus and Giroux, 1990.

Thurman, Susan. *The Everything Grammar and Style Book.* Avon, Mass: Adams Media Corporation, 2002.

Tully, Marianne. *Helping Students Revise Their Writing.* New York: Scholastic Professional Books, 1996.

Vacca, Richard, and Jo Anne Vacca. *Content Area Reading, 8th ed.* Boston: Allyn and Bacon, 2004.

Wong, Janet S. *You Have to Write.* New York: Simon & Schuster Children's Publishing, 2002.

Writers Inc. Lexington, Mass: Write Source, D.C. Heath and Company, 1996.

Zemelman, S., H. Daniels, and A. Hyde. *Best Practice: New Standards for Teaching and Learning in America's Schools. 2nd ed.* Portsmouth, NH: Heinemann, 1998.

Web sites:

www.askjeeves.com

www.cnr.colostate.edu/careers/fisherybiocareeroverview

www.enchantedlearning.com

www.fmnh.org/exhibits/exhibit_sites/wis/activities

www.pueblo.gsa.gov/cic_text/food/food-pyramid/main.htm

www.sandiegozoo.org/kids/job_profiles

www.scilinks.org